Embracing
the
Broken

Embracing the Broken

LETTING GO OF PERFECTION & LIVING BY THE POWER OF CHRIST'S GRACE

TIFFANY WEBSTER

Author of "Perfect Lie" and Founder of Evergreen

CFI

AN IMPRINT OF CEDAR FORT, INC.
SPRINGVILLE, UTAH

ISBN 13: 978-1-4621-2065-9

Published by CFI, an imprint of Cedar Fort, Inc.
2373 W. 700 S., Springville, UT 84663
Distributed by Cedar Fort, Inc., www.cedarfort.com

LIBRARY OF CONGRESS CATALOGING-IN-PUBLICATION DATA
Names: Webster, Tiffany, 1985- author.
Title: Embracing the broken / by Tiffany Webser.
Description: Springville, UT : CFI, An Imprint of Cedar Fort, Inc., [2017] |
   Includes bibliographical references and index.
Identifiers: LCCN 2017027673 (print) | LCCN 2017032885 (ebook) | ISBN
   9781462128174 (ebook) | ISBN 9781462120659 (pbk. : alk. paper)
Subjects: LCSH: Christian life--Mormon authors. | Perfectionism (Personality
   trait)--Religious aspects. | Guilt--Religious aspects.
Classification: LCC BX8656 (ebook) | LCC BX8656 .W43 2017 (print) | DDC
   248.4/89332--dc23
LC record available at https://lccn.loc.gov/2017027673

Cover design by Kinsey Beckett
Back cover design by Jeff Harvey
Cover design © 2017 by Cedar Fort, Inc.
Edited by Katy Watkins and Kaitlin Barwick
Typeset by Kaitlin Barwick

Printed in the United States of America

10 9 8 7 6 5 4 3 2 1

Printed on acid-free paper

DEDICATED TO MY FIFTEEN-YEAR-OLD SELF

*You are enough,
and you always have been.*

PRAISE FOR

Embracing the Broken

Embracing the Broken is one of the most deeply personal books I've ever read. Tiffany's writing is real, raw, and unafraid. You'll find inspiring and divine truths on every page.

—JASON F. WRIGHT, *New York Times* bestselling author of *The Wednesday Letters* and *Christmas Jars*

Reading *Embracing the Broken* is like having an uplifting and authentic conversation with a wise friend. Tiff's story of overcoming unrealistic expectations of perfection is candid, riveting, and relevant to any Latter-day Saint reader. Take the journey with her—you'll be glad you did.

—HANK SMITH, PhD, author of *Be Happy*

Embracing the Broken has given me a new perspective. Tiffany has rephrased the very same doctrine I have always known to be true in a way that has completely renewed my relationship with Christ. She has exposed her heart and heartache in this book so that all can apply a new understanding of Christ's role in our lives. Truly, in sharing her most tender trials and triumphs, Tiffany is walking side by side with Christ and giving us all a refreshing example of how we may be made whole in Him.

—SANDRA TURLEY, Broadway actress and inspirational speaker

Contents

INTRODUCTION

God Uses Broken Things

God uses broken things.
It takes broken soil to produce a crop,
broken clouds to give rain,
broken grain to give bread,
broken bread to give strength.
It is the broken alabaster box that
gives forth perfume.
It is Peter, weeping bitterly,
who returns to greater power than ever.

—Vance Havner[1]

Have you ever felt broken? Have you ever felt discouraged by your weaknesses and flaws? Have you ever feared that you'll never be enough? Yeah, me too.

Are you exhausted, frantic, or anxious? Measuring yourself by perfection? Suffocated by busyness? Wondering how you could possibly do more or be more? Yeah, that *was* me too.

Can I tell you a secret? It's OK that you feel broken. It's OK that you feel weak. In fact, having weakness is a crucial part of God's plan. But guess what? It's not OK that you don't feel enough, and it's not OK that you wonder if you ever will be. Because you already are. Wherever you are, however broken or flawed you feel, no matter how many mistakes you've made—you're enough! Do you know why? Because Jesus Christ is enough. And right now, in this moment, He will take you exactly how you are—every last piece of you. I know this because He took me at my lowest point, at a time when I felt shattered, worthless, and hopeless.

To those of you who are not of the LDS faith, I hope you know that this book is for you too! My experiences and some of my vocabulary come from my LDS background, but I hope you know that I also wrote this book thinking about you. I know Satan's lie of perfectionism doesn't just affect those of my faith, but all of us who are united in Christ. How thankful I am for you, for anyone and everyone who loves Jesus. I pray that you can feel the love of your Savior in these pages and that you can feel the power of Christ's grace working for your good.

If I'm being honest, I wish we could have this conversation over lunch. I'd give you a big hug and introduce myself. I'd ask you to tell me about all that you are. Your heart, your worries, your joys and fears. I'm sure we'd become fast friends, and I would tell you to call me Tiff. Who knows, maybe that will happen (I hope it does), but if not, know that I'm writing these words thinking about you and praying for you.

I know my story isn't the same as yours. You may not struggle with the chains of perfectionism, glorified busyness, lack of self-worth, chronic illness, or infertility—your journey may be completely different. That's OK, because this book really isn't about me. It's about Him. How He saved me from the depths of darkness and how He can do the same for you! No matter your story, your brokenness, weakness, or sins, He can change you, help you, and strengthen you, for that's what He has done for me. Christ took my anxious, exhausting, fear-based life and transformed it into a life of peace, wholeness, and joy. A life that's now lived intentionally, day by day, in His grace.

NOTE

1. Vance Havner, *Hearts Afire: Light on Successful Soul Winning* (Westwood, NJ: Fleming H. Revell, 1952), 76.

PART ONE

The Chains of Perfection

ONE

Perfectionism Is Born

I sat there staring at my race car on the wall. Everyone's cars had moved but mine, and I hated it. I was in third grade, and we were learning times tables. My teacher had created a large-scale racetrack that spanned the walls of our classroom, and every student was given a race car that represented how fast they could complete a sheet of multiplication problems without missing one. It had been a month, and there sat my car alone at the beginning. It hadn't moved an inch. OK, fine, it wasn't alone. It was there with two other cars, but I had dismissed both of them because they belonged to two kids in the class who had an innate anger toward school and who seemed couldn't care less if their cars moved, let alone if they even tried to do their work to begin with.

I'm sure I had felt this awful emotion before—but this is the first clear, vivid memory that I have of this feeling. It's the first of what would become many times where I felt "it," the shame, panic, and heartache of not measuring up and not being "enough." And it hurt.

The teacher passed out our daily times table sheet again. "Ready, set, go!" I hurried through it, trying so hard not to miss one. "TIME." We dropped our pencils and my teacher began calling off the answers. I started to get anxious. *So far so good. Only a few left. . . .* I was holding my breath.

"4 x 5 = 20"

"2 × 3 = 6"
"6 × 3 = 18"
"7 × 8 = 56"

My heart dropped. I immediately got a big lump in my throat. I didn't want to cry. *Please don't cry.* The teacher's voice faded and I remember the only thing I could hear was my heart pounding and my mind pleading with my eyes to hold back the tears. *Of course it was 56. Why did I put 35?*

"OK! If you got 100 percent and your time improved, go ahead and move your car to the next track."

I held my head down while large tears dropped onto my paper. I hated the tears. I wanted to hide. I pulled myself together and managed to make it through the rest of the day until I got home and saw my mom. She's my safe place. Always has been, and always will be. She's loved me through the darkest of times and cheered me on through the best. A million people can ask me how I am, and with a big smile I can answer "good." But with my mom, all walls come down, every single time. They always have. I sat there sobbing in her arms, telling her how hard I had tried and how embarrassed I was.

"I'm the dumbest one in class!"

My mom sat there holding me, saying all the right things that a mother should say, but I didn't listen. Nothing was settling my heart, and my hurt was turning into anger. I was mad. I hated that feeling and I never wanted to feel it again. Ever.

The next day my mom and I met with my teacher after school. She really was the kindest lady and one of my favorite elementary teachers. To this day I know she only hoped to help and make me the best she could. After explaining my frustration and sadness, she graciously gave me a large stack of multiplication sheets to take home for practice. For the following weeks, I spent hours and hours making my way through the stack. I'd race the timer, race my dad, and then race my mom. I would do them after school and before bed. I was determined. I'd like to blame genes, but I'm sure I would have come this way no matter what: competitive. It runs deep in me, and you could say this incident may have been the spark that woke the beast.

I practiced, and practiced, and practiced. And you know what? My car started moving, and it started moving fast. In fact, by the end of the year, it had moved to the very front of the track. I was rewarded with a special lunch date with my teacher and the only other two kids who were able to do a full sheet of multiplication problems in less than two minutes.

Now, I know what you may be thinking, "Tiffany, this is a great story! A story of triumph, hard work, and dedication. A story with a good ending." OK, sure. It is. And don't get me wrong, I'm a big believer in the power of hard work and perseverance. But this story? It isn't about that. It's about something much deeper. It's about something much more. Because that moment, as rewarding as it was, wasn't born out of hope. It was born out of fear—fear of failing, fear of not being enough, fear of not fitting in, and fear of never measuring up. For the next twenty years, fear sat in the driver's seat behind all that I did. And let me tell you—fear isn't that great. It's kinda awful, and it almost ruined my life.

I was lucky enough to be born to parents who loved the Lord. They raised me in the gospel of Jesus Christ where the motto "choose the right" became the measuring stick to everything I did and the imprint that laid visibly on my heart and soul. I'm passionate and stubborn, but my heart is tender. I'm a people pleaser and empathizer. I hate seeing people sad, and I hate letting others down. I've always been this way. You know what I mean? I believe we each came to this earth with certain attributes and characteristics embedded so deep within us that there is no other explanation to why we are the way we are except for the truth that we are spiritual beings who have existed forever. If you are a parent, you may understand what I'm talking about. Shortly after having a child, it becomes obvious that they came to earth with attributes that you, as their parent, couldn't have possibly taught them at such a young age. Some kids come running out of the womb with a fierce determination to conquer the world. Others are calm, patient, and easygoing. Some a little more stubborn, independent, and fearless.

Me? Well I was inherently what you would call a "good girl." Not to be confused with "perfect," but rather I was naturally born with an eager spirit to do and be good. I didn't enjoy getting in trouble, and for the most part I tried hard to be obedient. I remember specifically the first time I lied to my mom. I was in fifth grade, and I was struggling with some health issues and insecurities of being "bigger" than all my friends. These struggles made me keenly aware of how much junk food I ate, and my sweet mother knew I was trying to eat healthier.

One day while doing the laundry, my mom found two full-sized candy wrappers inside my pant pockets. I was standing there, and she innocently asked me if they were both mine. There were those feelings again: shame, panic, embarrassment. I looked at her and told her that one was mine, but the other was a friend's who had "asked me to take her trash for her."

I was also gifted with the ability to harbor immense guilt. I carried that dumb lie with me for five years until I was fifteen. We had had a lesson on honesty in Sunday School, and I came home crying to my mom confessing that both those candy wrappers had indeed been mine, and that I was so sorry I had lied to her! I then begged for her forgiveness. She obviously forgave me, and today we both laugh at my . . . well, I don't even know how you would label that. But every time we talk about it, we laugh.

Needless to say I didn't get in trouble very often. Not because I was "just so good," but because I had a real fear of messing up or doing something wrong. Even the slightest disappointed look sent me spiraling. It's almost unexplainable, but it was real. Like I said, I was born a "good girl."

Don't be deceived, this doesn't mean that I didn't have struggles. Oh no, I had plenty of those. I was 100 percent awkward and insecure, plus I grew what felt like one thousand times faster than all my friends. Today, I stand at a solid five foot eleven inches. I don't remember the words *petite* or *small* ever following me anywhere. As a young girl, this can completely wreak havoc on your self-esteem.

I was cut from the school choir, *twice*, and I was told I didn't get the part of Clara in the *Nutcracker* in third grade because they needed a girl who was small enough for the prince to lift in the air. Then there was that time I misjudged the velocity of the playground slide, and I found myself lying in a giant puddle. With mud covering my backside, I rushed inside to call my mom. As I walked to the office I heard the fifth-graders making their way to lunch. I panicked and pressed my backside up against the wall. Hoping, praying that they wouldn't notice me. I mean, maybe they wouldn't notice a second-grader pressed up against the wall, shuffling to the office with a trail of mud behind her?

I won't even mention the time the entire school saw my bright-green underwear during a school performance. So, yes. I definitely had plenty of problems without breaking the rules. I know most of this is 100 percent worse in my head. Those who knew me at a young age have completely different views of who I was, but this was my reality. I was a tall, awkward girl who feared failing and desperately yearned to be enough. And in a world that tells us to cover up even the slightest flaw on our face, this can be terribly hard. I hated that feeling—that fear and sadness that comes from feeling like you are "less than," that you don't belong, and that you don't measure up. But it's been there, staring me in the face since I was young.

At its root, perfectionism isn't really about a deep love of being meticulous.

> It's about fear. Fear of making a mistake. Fear of disappointing others. Fear of failure.
>
> —Michael Law[1]

And this fear—it didn't just stop at me feeling like I didn't have worth. No, because fear feeds fear. And fear and I, we developed a tight relationship. I knew it well at an early age. It's cruel, with the ability to suck joy out of every situation—family vacations, school, relationships, having a child, marriage, careers, the world. It's right there, every second, desperately trying with all its might to hologram the worst possible scenario that could happen. Nudging and reminding you of the costs and pain to every situation: ATV rides, lake trips, sleepovers, the dark. When my parents would go out of town, I was certain they wouldn't come back. It didn't matter what it was, there was fear, causing me all kinds of anxiety while breathing toxic darkness into every aspect of my life.

———

Sure, your fear may not look like mine; fear has endless masks and comes in all shapes and sizes. It has different voices and different levels. But in the end, it affects us all.

Fear is everything that God isn't, and it is the catalyst to each and every weapon that Satan uses against us. Fear is the parent of shame and the driving force behind anything that keeps us away from God. "Fear . . . is a principal weapon in the arsenal that Satan uses to make mankind unhappy."[2] It always has been.

GUILT ➡ FEAR ➡ SHAME

Let's go back to the Garden of Eden, shall we? Adam and Eve are living "unashamed" in their nakedness in the Garden of Eden with two commandments that they are to obey:

1. To not partake of the fruit from the tree of the knowledge of good and evil
2. To multiply and replenish the earth

Then, who shows up? Satan, tempting and trying both Adam and Eve to partake of the fruit that they had been forbidden to eat. The story unfolds as Adam and Eve become conflicted, and in temptation they both end up partaking of the fruit from the tree of knowledge of good and evil. Naturally, this choice brings with it guilt, as guilt is the direct consequence and feeling we get from disobeying God's commandments. What follows next is extremely important. Satan, knowing exactly what has transpired, then feeds fear into Adam and Eve's natural feelings of guilt. This fear then becomes shame. And that shame drives Adam and Eve to hide themselves from God.

> And they knew that they had been naked. . . .
> And they heard the voice of the Lord God . . . and Adam and his wife went to hide themselves from the presence of the Lord God. . . .
> And I, the Lord God, called unto Adam, and said unto him: Where goest thou?
> And he [Adam] said: I heard thy voice in the garden, and I was afraid, because I beheld that I was naked, and I hid myself." (Moses 4:13–16)

In only a few short verses of scripture, we go from an Adam and Eve who are unashamed of their nakedness to an Adam and Even who have now spiraled from guilt to fear and to shame and hiding.

Growing up, I didn't understand the difference between *guilt* and *shame*. One of my favorite contributors in helping me understand this topic more clearly is expert researcher and author Brené Brown. Brown has spent years studying vulnerability, courage, worthiness, and shame. She states:

> I believe that there is a profound difference between shame and guilt. I believe that guilt is adaptive and helpful—it's holding something we've done or failed to do up against our values and feeling psychological discomfort.

I define shame as the intensely painful feeling or experience of believing that we are flawed and therefore unworthy of love and belonging—something we've experienced, done, or failed to do makes us unworthy of connection.[3]

In the context of the gospel, we know that guilt stems from truth. It's a natural emotion that comes as a consequence of sin. For "the Lord cannot look upon sin with the least degree of allowance" (D&C 1:31). Hence, there must be some sort of emotion that motivates us to be better, to change and to repent. However, guilt should never keep us from God. The purpose of guilt is to turn us back to Christ and back to our God, having hope in Them because we know that through Them we can become more. Guilt should be a healthy emotion that brings change.

Our sins and weaknesses should never define us. When guilt turns us away from God, when it tells us that we are unworthy or that we need to hide our brokenness and flaws—you can absolutely know that Satan has stepped in, that he has fed our guilt with fear and shame, and that he is doing everything he can to keep us hidden and distanced from God (and not just God, but from all and any connection that he can).

> For we wrestle not against flesh and blood, but against principalities, against powers, against the rulers of the darkness of this world, against spiritual wickedness in high places. (Ephesians 6:12)

I hate giving the adversary any more attention than I already have, and I hate acknowledging him, but I believe it's crucial. This war we are facing, it's not against each other or against God—it's against him. Satan knows us. He knew us before we came here. He knows our weaknesses and our inadequacies. He knows that we chose Christ, and he hates us for that.

Satan is miserable and will do anything to destroy our happiness and light. Everything that he does is driven from one core mission and goal: to keep us away from our Savior, Jesus Christ. Eating disorders, drugs, pornography, bullying, immorality, lying—sure, these are all different behaviors and different lures. But ultimately, they all have one purpose and are each driven from a place of fear, shame, and pain. Perfectionism? It's no different. At the end of the day, it's just another lure disguised in beautiful wrapping that seems harmless. But of course, that's how each of his lures start, clipping themselves into us carefully while we aren't looking.

You remember the famous frog analogy, right? In order to kill a frog using water, you have to start by placing it in water that it's comfortable in. If you immediately set it into boiling water, it would jump right out. So rather you set it in water that seems pleasant and unharmful. Then slowly you turn up the heat, one degree at a time. Eventually, the water is boiling, and before the frog realizes what is happening, it's too late. He's gone. Actually, why are we allowed to tell that story to our kids? It's a little more graphic than I realized. But it's real. And it's true.

I remember brushing this lesson off, thinking that it only applied to addictive behavior such as pornography, drugs, or alcohol. But it doesn't. Satan has a tactic for each of us and little did I know that while I was busy brushing it off, I had actually fallen into my own pot of comfortable water. I mean, the scriptures do tell us to "be ye therefore perfect," right? (See Matthew 5:48.) Plus, all I was trying to do is be highly successful at everything I did. "And now the serpent was more subtle than any beast of the field which I, the Lord God had made" (Moses 4:5). Perfectionism was an easy fit, and Satan knew it.

"Drugs and alcohol aren't gonna work as well on this one. Let's tell her she isn't good enough, bind her with perfectionism, and shame her into hiding. She'll never see it coming!"

NOTES

1. "Michael Law Quotes," Goodreads, accessed June 21, 2017, https://www .goodreads.com/author/quotes/664650.Michael_Law.
2. Howard W. Hunter, "An Anchor to the Souls of Men," *Ensign*, October 1993.
3. Brené Brown, "Shame v. Guilt," Brenebrown.com, posted January 14, 2013, accessed June 14, 2017, http://brenebrown.com/2013/01/14/2013114shame -v-guilt-html.

TWO

The Voice of a Perfectionist

Mom! I can't find my basketball shoes or my homework! Can you bring me lunch today? I'm so sorry, I just don't have time to make it. Ugh! I'm so stressed. . . . Where are my basketball shoes?! I have a student council meeting at lunch, and then I have a yearbook deadline that needs to be done during fourth period. After school I have basketball practice, and then I have to get back to the gym to help set up for Junior Prom because National Honor Society is in charge of it and I haven't done enough service hours this semester! Oh, and I have a big chemistry test tomorrow that I haven't studied for, and if I don't get a 94, I'll lose my A! Dang it! Where are my shoes?!"

With a pure heart and innocent intentions, I was out to create the perfect life for myself. I was ambitious, determined, and driven. I wanted to be like my Savior, have a successful life, and make the world a better place. I was a constant tornado at a fast-paced rate, destroying anything that got in my way. Once I was hooked into perfectionism, I began filling my life with every extracurricular activity possible. I had this urge to not only be good at everything I did, but also to be the best. Piano lessons, basketball, softball, volleyball, student council, straight A's, yearbook staff, National Honors Society, Church callings, service projects, AP classes—my schedule was overflowing with each priority seeping into the other and overlapping.

My mother deserves a million gold stars for her endless patience and for keeping me from losing any more of my fragile sanity. My mind was always moving to the next task and I was never really present to the one I was in. I'm naturally a forgetful person, but because of the load I was carrying and the checklist that I had given myself, my life was out of control. I lost count of how many times I had to call my mom in the middle of the day because I forgot a sports bra for basketball practice.

I wasn't aware at the time, but I was addicted to being busy and my worth was being measured by the amount of items on my checklist, including how well I did them. There was no room for error, no room for flaw. It didn't matter how well I performed or how many activities I was involved in, there was always more to be done, something I could do better, or something I was lacking.

On the outside, it looked nothing like this. I was a regional softball MVP, held state records for pitching, made first team all-state, was a straight-A student, a yearbook editor, and a member of the Junior Class Council. I was successful, put together, and on the outside I seemed happy. On the inside I was a nervous wreck. The fear of not being enough haunted my every move and I had a heightened awareness to everything I wasn't. If someone else achieved something more than I had, then I was a failure. My thinking became skewed and my perspective distorted. The only way I knew how to handle my failures and insecurities was to work harder and be harder on myself, because perfectionism doesn't give room for growing. It expects perfect results, every day, all the time.

I remember a specific incident my Freshman year. It was softball season, and we had a game in Cedar City, Utah. The wind was vicious, and it was raining and cold. I don't know if you've played softball in rainy, cold weather, but it's not fun. And it's hard. I was pitching, and we were up 14–0. My fingers were frozen, my arm was starting to cramp, and it was getting difficult to control the ball. At the top of the fifth inning, I walked the first batter. Then the second. Then the third. And then, yes, the fourth, bringing a girl home to score.

I was furious! How could I?! I had never even walked two people in a row, let alone walk someone home to score. (The audacity!) I was extremely upset at myself. Telling myself all sorts of awful things in my head. Holding back tears. Luckily I had a wise coach. He called a time-out and jogged out to the mound where the entire team huddled around.

"Tiff." He looked me in the eyes.

Ugh! I had failed. I wanted to cry.

"Four walks in a row."

"I know coach. I'm trying, and I'm just so sorry. I won't let it happen again!" Tears were definitely streaming down my face by then. (I was a fifteen-year-old girl, so don't judge too harshly.)

"Well, I can see why you'd be so upset. I mean, four walks in a row, that just isn't like you." I hung my head. He continued, "Tiff, it's miserable and cold out here, and the score *is* 14–1. I think we *might* be OK." He was smiling, and the entire team laughed. I took a deep breath in and then laughed. Well, I cry-laughed, which ended in a loud snort. But I laughed and we finished the game.

As I write this I can't help but shake my head in disbelief. How could I have been so hard on myself? Why was I so focused on performing perfectly that I couldn't give myself a break? I knew it was cold. I knew given the circumstances I had every reason to give myself slack. But I wouldn't allow it. My head told me things like, *You should still be able to pitch perfectly. I don't care about the circumstances; a great athlete would push through and still perform at their best. No excuses. No mistakes.*

Sure, this story is my ninth-grade version, but this self-abuse and unrealistic expectation became my reality.

I don't care that you've never been to college, you shouldn't have missed that deadline and you should know how to handle the registration and admissions process.

I don't care that you were up all night with a sick child and never slept, you should still be able to meet your work deadlines.

I don't care that your husband moved to another state for work and you're left packing the house. You pull yourself together, put a smile on, and get to work.

I don't care that your leg hurts. You get your butt out of bed and you go running anyway.

No excuses. No mistakes.

> Perfectionism is a self-destructive and addictive belief system that fuels this primary thought: If I look perfect and do everything perfectly, I can avoid the painful feelings of shame, judgment and blame.
>
> —Brené Brown[1]

Perfectionism is like an inner demon that we think is motivating us to be the best, do our best. But in reality, it's destroying who we really are.

Making us slaves and imprisoning us to a life full of anxiety, stress, and exhaustion. Like I mentioned before, perfectionism isn't born out of hope of all that we can become, it's born out of fear. Allowing every broken piece we have to grow that fear. Fear that we aren't enough. Pain that we won't measure up.

So shamefully, we hide. We run. We do all we can to keep every last piece of brokenness inside us, hidden away.

If (*when*) my weakness or failures showed, I'd lose it. My stress level would go from a one to a ten instantly, and my anxiety would shoot through the roof.

PERFECTIONISM FEARS FAILING

When I entered college, I was on a full academic and athletic scholarship. In the first three years of college, I played two full years of softball and one year of basketball, served on the Institute council, was VP of publicity for my student government, was an assistant high school softball and basketball coach . . . and on and on.

School was never easy for me. I'm not a natural test taker, and I have to study extremely long for information to stick. My husband can read something once and remember it forever. Me? Not so much. So on top of all my extracurricular activities, I was staying up late so I had enough time to study.

Once I entered my third year of college, my classes were getting extremely difficult. I was being pulled in too many directions, and my mind was fatigued. Slowly, my grades started slipping, and I honestly didn't know how to handle it. I had a certain class that was particularly challenging, and I remember that the end of the quarter was near and I had a C.

It was the last week of class, and I was on my way to take my last test that would determine my final grade. I feared I didn't know the information well enough. In fact, I knew I didn't know what I needed to in order to pull off a higher grade. I pulled into the parking lot with the intention to be on time. However, the fear of failing the test and possibly losing my academic scholarship was too much for my mind to handle. I sat there, sobbing, not being able to breathe. I was spiraling into a panic attack, and I couldn't stop it. If you have experienced panic attacks, you know what I am talking about. If not, well, count your blessings.

I couldn't do it. I couldn't get out of the car. For more than thirty minutes I sat in my Jeep, experiencing an extreme panic attack that felt as though it would never end.

There is nothing wrong with a C. And I know that seems a little ridiculous and dramatic at the effect it had on me. But I was suffering greatly from the chains of perfection and anxiety, and incidents like this weren't unusual, especially when I was trying to face an area of my life that I had fallen short in.

As I think back and remember all that I use to demand of myself, my heart aches. In high school, after a four-hour-long softball practice, I use to make one of my best friends (who happened to be my catcher) or my mom stay with me and catch for me as I relentlessly pitched for another two hours, never quitting until I ended with the "perfect" pitch.

If I missed more than just a few shots in my basketball game, you'd find me shooting for hours after practice, doing the same shot over and over.

Don't get me wrong—hard work is essential. It's an honorable trait. But nothing about the abuse I was putting myself through was honorable. It was destructive.

> Perfectionism is self-abuse of the highest order.
>
> —Anne Wilson Schaef[2]

And this is how I lived every day, month, and year. Repeating the same cycle of guilt and shame over and over again.

I'd create a long list of goals and expectations. Then I'd hustle with every ounce of energy I had to perfect these goals. I'd fall short, run into obstacles, experience failure, which led to me feeling worthless. I'd then become overwhelmed with anxiety and fear that I would never accomplish my goals. This was always followed by depression and hopelessness, then anger and self-abuse, renewed by an unhealthy determination to never, ever let myself feel like this again, determined that this time, I wasn't going to fail!

But of course I would fail. Every time. Because those goals, those expectations were impossible. Plus, they only got bigger, and the vice of perfection only got tighter. I wanted the big dreams, the successful life: a beautiful home, big yard, five kids, and a strong, skinny body. I wanted to be an earlier riser, take my kids on adventures, be a professional photographer, and never miss scripture study.

Thinking about the slippery slope of this vice gives me chills. I thought my intentions were righteous and good. I wanted to be just like my Savior, live a successful life, make the world a better place, and be a good Christian, wife, mother, sister, friend, and daughter.

I was a people pleaser. Because of course, to be perfect like Christ, I needed to serve the way He did, constantly showing love and kindness to everyone. I needed everyone to be happy with me, and I didn't know how to say no. If someone needed help, I'd be there, because that's what a perfect person does. We say yes, to everything and everyone. Or at least I did. Hurting someone's feelings killed me, and I never wanted to let anyone down. I wanted others to know they could count on me. And they did. I didn't have any boundaries, so people asked for help—a lot. And I said yes, almost every time.

Deep down, I knew there was something wrong. The load of perfectionism is heavy. It's a full-time job trying to keep all your pieces in their "proper" place, while also saying yes to everyone and every opportunity possible. But I wanted to help. I wanted people to know I loved them. I wanted to be successful. I wanted to be good. And I *was*. I had set a strong precedent that I *was* all of these things. I was a good girl. I chose the right. And teachers, coaches, and parents would constantly praise me for my actions.

"I don't know how you do it all, Tiff. You are so amazing. So incredible. So strong."

Comments like this fed my self-esteem. I had attached my self-esteem to my worth, and I believed I had value as long as people thought highly of me. And as long as I was strong, highly involved, and making the right choices, people did praise me. Parents knew I was a good kid and would often encourage their own children to be friends with me.

"Tiff, you keep an eye on everyone. Make sure they all stay in line."

"I'm not worried about my daughter. If she's with you, I know she won't do anything wrong."

Is there anything wrong with these statements? No. However, when they are constantly coming at you, the responsibility can become taxing. It's a big responsibility as a teenager to feel like you are the strength that helps others make right choices. This isn't actual truth; we all have our agency. And I'm sure people didn't actually depend on me to make the right choice. However, this was my reality. In my mind, I couldn't mess up—at all. Too many people depended on me.

With each year that passed, the pressure to *always* make the right choice seemed to be getting harder and harder. Sure, I didn't always keep it together in high school, but I had figured out how to keep straight A's and be successful in about all that I did. I don't say this out of arrogance either. I worked extremely hard at it. But by the time I was a senior, I felt like I had a good hand on juggling it all.

College. Yeah, different ball game. Everything amplified times one hundred. Friends started making wrong hard decisions. School was a lot harder. Sports were now a job. Yet there I stayed, trying to "do it all" and "be it all." It became a lot of pressure, especially because I felt anything but perfect.

I may have been one of the best players in high school, but when you get to college, you are playing with *all* the best players from high school. It quickly became obvious that I was one of the weakest links on the team. Starting from the first day of practice, I had my work cut out for me. Most days were spent at the field, practicing an additional two hours after a four-or-five-hour team practice.

We had an assistant coach who could see that I was struggling. He took me under his wing and was determined to help me get better. We didn't come from the same faith, but he will forever be someone I cherish because of the life lessons he taught me.

However, he was hard on me. And I was hard on myself. I hated that I was "failing," that a sport that had always come so naturally to me was now something that was causing me so much frustration and heartache. I hated that I was weak. I hated those feelings of shame that would arise when I'd miss a pitch, strike out, or overthrow a base. The burden of keeping it all together was becoming heavier and heavier—especially because I *wasn't* keeping it all together.

One particular practice, I was having a hard day, and my coach started singling me out. We were doing infield practice, and I was at first base. He started going around the circle, slamming ground balls as hard as he could. There was never any mercy. His motto and goal was to ensure that we never faced competition harder than him.

He started at third base and made his way around the infield. There was no mercy and he was going full speed ahead. As he got to me, he got that look in his eye, and I knew I better strap it on. I sat there as he nailed ground balls right at my feet and then off to the side purposely making me dive onto dirt that felt like concrete. Balls were ricocheting off my glove, cleats, and shins. He didn't move on.

"Get the ball!" he screamed.

I could feel the frustration and anger building up inside me. I was flustered and knew the entire team was staring at me. I was missing ball after ball with only seconds between each hit. He didn't let up, hitting them to my right, to my left, and then right at my ankles.

"Get up! Now! Get it! I'm not going to stop until you get five in a row!"

I was being plastered, and it was breaking me. I dove after a ball in the dirt, and it hit my glove, barely rolling in. Immediately, I stood up as a ball came flying at my ankle. I put my glove down as fast as I could, but it hit the tip, slamming into my foot and rolling off the sideline.

"D— it!!!" I screamed. I was furious.

Everything stopped. Including the coach. Immediately, a roaring laugh fanned across the field. No one had ever heard me swear.

I tried to play it off, pretending to laugh. "Guys! It's not funny! I'm so pissed."

"Yeah, but Tiff, you never swear! You're basically perfect, and it's almost comical."

The coach looked at me with a slight grin and winked. He moved on to the next drill.

I'm not particularly proud of the fact that I swore, and especially that I continued to swear. Nor would I ever encourage anyone else to pick up this lame habit. But for me, it was a cry, a plea for help. The pressure of always saying the right thing, being the right thing, doing the right thing—I couldn't handle it. I guess, in a sense, it was my rebellious moment. I know, it sounds pretty pathetic, and it's a blessing I didn't decide to do something that would have been much more damaging—but still, it was real.

After practice, my coach found me and wrapped his arm around me.

"I'm sorry I pissed you off so badly today, and I'm sorry I made you swear. I wasn't easy on you, and I'm proud of you. You're a good sport, and I want you to know I'm only trying to make you better. Tougher. Stronger."

I smiled and said all the things I usually do. But deep down I was tired. I was angry. I felt broken, and I didn't even want to try to be perfect any more. I didn't want to be strong. I didn't want the pressure. I wanted out!

I'm lucky I had the testimony that I did. Growing up, I saw through family members and loved ones what happens when you chose to go against the commandments of God. I witnessed what happens when you choose the wrong friends, take your first drink, flirt with immorality, or simply stop going to church. Watching loved ones go through these experiences became real-life teaching moments for me at a time when the pressures of perfection felt too high—I knew that the alternative wasn't any better, but only worse.

However, this moment of "wanting out" has given me a better understanding to why someone would leave the gospel. It breaks my heart. But when you misunderstand the truth and you are deceived by this lie curated around perfection—I understand why it would appear easier to leave. It *is* too much. But that's what Satan does. He corners you into believing that there are only two options:

Forever keep carrying the chains of perfection, until one day you finally make it to the promised land and you are miraculously living a life free of flaw.

Free yourself from the expectation of perfection, abandon your faith and standards, and leave the gospel.

At least this is how I felt. I hated how heavy and chaotic my life felt trying to strive for perfection. I was tired of never feeling enough. Yet I had watched closely what the alternative was. I had too many family members choose the second. I knew what would happen if I abandoned the gospel. I definitely didn't want that. I could see how the gospel should and does bring happiness. I knew, because of my parents, that leaving wasn't the choice I wanted to make. So I stayed, not knowing how to get out of the rut I was in, chained to perfection.

NOTES

1. Brené Brown, "Perfectionism and Claiming Shame," Brenebrown.com, posted March 18, 2009, accessed June 14, 2017, http://brenebrown.com /2009/03/18/2009318perfectionism-and-claiming-shame-html.
2. Anne Wilson Shaef, *Meditations for Women Who Do Too Much*, rev. upd. ed. (New York: HarperOne, 2004), 27.

THREE

Marriage Will Fix It?

When I struggled with my imperfections and insecurities growing up, I'd dream of what it would be like to be married. Like most thirteen-year-old girls, I dreamed about how I'd meet my future husband. He would be this tall, athletic, football player, with dark hair and a sensitive side. Someone who could sing and was musically inclined, loved adventure, and worked as hard as I did. Someone who wanted to travel the world, who was going to be a successful doctor or lawyer. We would probably meet at BYU, after he had served a mission. While he was on his mission, I'm sure he would have been the assistant to the president and the leading baptizer. Everyone would love him, and people would always comment how I was the luckiest girl ever to be married to him.

It would be perfect.

Marriage seemed like the final destination, the "happily ever after." The key and answer to finally help me feel enough. How could it not be? For a girl who believed that boys would never like her. Who felt like she wasn't beautiful or worth enough to love. Surely having a boyfriend and especially a husband would fix all of this? How could I still be fearful of not being enough, when someone had chosen to be with me for eternity and who loved me with all of his heart? Yes. When I get married, I'll finally feel enough. Insert exaggerated eye roll and facepalm emoji.

Of course, in reality, nothing happened the way I thought it would.

Wes and I met in middle school. I was insecure and awkward with a full mouth of braces. Wes was tall, lanky, and fighting acne. You could say it was love at first sight! OK, not really. In fact, Wes doesn't even remember our first real interactions, although he humors me and pretends like it left a lasting mark on him the same way it did for me.

I came running into the school with only one minute to spare. It was game day and we were headed out of town for a weekend tournament. I was carrying my backpack, overnight duffle bag, my basketball gear, a bag of snacks, and a poster board that I needed for a science project, all while frantically (and awkwardly) running to class because I couldn't be late.

"Hey!" I could hear a voice behind me.

"Tiff! Hey, let me help you!"

I was a fourteen-year-old girl who was certain that boys didn't notice her, let alone would take the time to talk to her.

"You're going to be late, right? Let me help you."

He grabbed two of my bags and my science project and ran with me down the hall to our class. We walked in just as the bell rang.

"Umm. Wow. Thank you. That was—I just really—I was going to be late."

"Don't worry about it. I was happy to help. Good luck at your games this weekend."

"Yeah. OK. Thanks."

For a fourteen-year-old girl, kindness from a boy like this goes a long way. Apparently, being the fourteen-year-old boy who helped the girl doesn't quite leave the same impression. No, I had no idea that Wes would be the one. Nor would I have guessed that years later we would start dating. But you can guarantee that interaction has never left my mind. To feel noticed, to be helped—it goes a long way, especially for a girl who sat home for more prom nights than she actually went to.

For the rest of high school, Wes and I were both highly involved in our own lives, hardly crossing paths besides the occasional smile and wave in the hallway. My senior year of high school, my family moved into the same neighborhood as Wes's grandparents. His grandparents and I were in the same ward, and they quickly became aware of who I was. Wes's grandpa, Grandpa Jack, was a stubborn old man. He had a mean hard front, but deep down, you knew he had a good heart.

Grandpa Jack was the old man you would find at sporting events who would yell and cuss at every call an empire or referee made. He had a rough beginning, but he was a good grandpa, and he loved his grandkids. Grandpa Jack had been recruited to play professional baseball, and in his later days, he played fastpitch softball. When he found out that I was a softball pitcher, he quickly gained interest in me. He would pull me away from Sunday School or invite me to his home to look at his roses—just so we could talk softball, and he could share his glory days with me. I loved it.

Naturally as time went on, Grandpa Jack gained an interest in making sure that Wes and I became good friends. He would call Wes, asking him to drive him to my softball games, while simultaneously encouraging Wes to interact with me as much as possible. By the end of our senior year, Wes and I were hanging out almost every single day. There was some unseen connection that either of us could explain. We would talk for hours about anything and everything. We could talk all night and sometimes did. (Mom, we only broke curfew a few times, I promise.) Wes ended up being my first kiss and the first boy to ever tell me he loved me. We had plenty of eighteen-year-old drama, and everything about it wasn't perfect, but he was my best friend and always made me feel better, in every possible way.

However, if you were to ask me if I knew that we were going to get married, I would have told you no. On paper—well, my perfectionist paper—Wes didn't meet everything I thought I wanted. He was skinny and slower to motivate. He never did things that were rushed. Plus, there were about ten other nitpicky things about him that bothered me. He was a local boy, and I swore I would never marry anyone from high school. My perfectionist voice told me that we weren't the "perfect match," that we especially didn't look perfect together. I had a way of finding the slightest flaw in myself, and when you are looking for a spouse, well, you start finding those flaws in them too.

After our first semester of college, Wes was called to serve in the Pennsylvania Philadelphia Mission. We wrote for a few months, but eventually he knew he wanted to give all of his time and efforts to God, and, well, I needed to date. And I did.

While I was dating, there seemed to be plenty of guys who seemed to be a much better fit to my perfectionist checklist—guys that played football, guys that were pushers and perfectionists like me. Yet no matter how many nice guys I dated, Wes was always there in the back of my mind. And I missed him.

Our friendship ran deep, and no one seemed to make me feel the way he did. Wes had kind eyes and a good soul. As my best friend, he had seen me at my absolute worst, and loved me before I had even the slightest confidence in myself. He was home. Our souls knew each other, and as cliché as it is, I knew that we were meant for each other.

Wes came home from his mission in April of 2006, and we were married August of that year. It was fast. But it was perfect—well, perfect for a moment.

There is no doubt, Wes loved me with all of his heart. He wanted to be with me. I knew that. I knew that we were right for each other. We still are. However, at the end of the day we were and are two different individuals, completely flawed and broken in our own ways. We were both growing, changing, and trying to make it.

Wes had always been the one to make me happy. He knew what to say to make me feel loved. Maybe it was because we were young, or ignorant, but somehow I believed that marriage would be the answer to happiness, that because I had someone who wanted to be with me forever, I'd have someone who always made me happy. This is also a lie. No one, not even our spouse, can be responsible for our happiness.

In just a few short months of marriage, I found myself still lacking self-esteem and still feeling like I didn't measure up. It didn't matter how many times Wes told me that he loved me, or how many times he praised my efforts, I didn't feel it. And, once again I questioned my worth. The fear of not being perfect was resurfacing, but this time at a more intense level than before. Because now it wasn't just *me*. It was *us*, and it was *him*. Now that we were married, Wes was an extension of who I was, a part of me. Whatever he did, however successful he was, it became a direct reflection on me as well.

Wes is a movie lover. He always has been. He can quote any and every movie that he's ever seen. When we were dating, he would always try and get me to sit down and watch a movie with him. He constantly told me that before we die, he was going to help me learn how to relax, to just sit and be. To be able to sit for two hours watching a movie, cuddling, not doing anything. Just being.

I'd laugh and brush it off. And, well, while we were dating I found myself more obliged to try and do what he wanted, so occasionally I would sit down and watch. But I was never just watching. I was always working on my computer or doing something "productive" while we watched.

Sitting still for two hours watching a movie seemed like the biggest waste of time. With all the dreams, checklists, and expectations I had on myself, I didn't have time to watch a movie. And really, neither did Wes. (Or so I believed.)

I have a deep love for others. Forgiveness and kindness usually come easy to me. Even at a young age, I've always believed in seeing the very best in people. My parents taught me by their example the importance of never judging and to always give people the benefit of the doubt. This was easily how I treated others, but never myself. No. And now, just shortly after marriage, I was bleeding my perfectionist ways onto my husband and became extremely hard on everything that he did.

You didn't study for your test? You could have done better at this. How could you be OK with getting a B? Did you really try your best? Don't you think you should eat better? Exercise more? Did you even read your scriptures today? We need to try harder at being better!

I was a pusher, always pushing to the next thing. Never satisfied, never content. (Again, pushing ourselves isn't bad, but when you push yourself with no room for failure or flaws, it becomes unhealthy and destructive to you and your spouse.)

Often I would sit down with a long list in my mind of everything that Wes and I could be doing better. This scenario always started with me first asking him, "What are a few things that I could do better as a wife?" I sincerely wanted to know and was ready to take on whatever he said.

"Tiff. There is absolutely nothing that you could do better. I love you for who you are. Always."

"Wes, there has to be something. Do I need to cook more? Be kinder?"

"Nope. You're doing a great job."

"Ugh. So you don't care? You are just fine with how things are. *We* need to be better. I want to be better. I know I have a lot of things I need to be better at. Just tell me everything else I need to work on so I can try harder to be better at those things."

He would sit there staring at me, not knowing what to say. I would get mad and frustrated that he wasn't "motivated to change." Then I would rattle off everything that I felt like he needed to be better at, while of course justifying it because I would then rattle off everything else that I needed to be better at as well.

Truthfully, it breaks my heart. I've almost deleted this chapter multiple times. Obviously, I'm pulling out the hardest parts of this burden. Was our marriage always like this? Absolutely not.

Eight months into marriage, I had brain surgery for a condition called Arnold Chiari malformation. My health has been a struggle most of my life, and Wes has walked beside me, helping me and carrying me. We've absolutely had moments of joy, and we have weathered some hard, hard things together, learning and growing alongside each other. However, for years I also yoked my sickness to him as well, expecting him to meet my unrealistic expectations.

And for the sake of trying to help even one newly married couple out there, I'm willing to share even the hardest parts.

I had chained my husband to my own shackles of perfection, and it sickens me. I didn't know I was doing this. I thought marriage would change how I felt about my worth, but it didn't. Because not even a spouse, or a child can change your worth, only Christ can.

And there I was, newly married, believing that I needed to be perfect, that Wes needed to be perfect, that we needed to be perfect together. This perfection that I'm talking about isn't in any way righteous, and it extends far beyond a Christian checklist. This perfection is what the world demands of us. A flawless, hustling, become-a-millionaire-by-the-age-of-twenty-five kind of perfection. The world breeds it into us before we can even walk, and we then breed it into each other as we relentlessly try to be more than the next guy.

What kind of occupation will make us the most money? How much college credit can we finish before we are done with high school? How soon can we get into our first home?

We are constantly competing and scrambling to climb the ladder of success.

I don't think we mean to do this—at least I didn't. I wasn't trying to get sucked into this tornado. I just honestly believed that in order to have a successful life, Wes and I needed to get from point A to point B as fast as we could. I had big dreams for us: retiring early, going on missions, building a beautiful home that our children could grow up in and that all the neighborhood kids could gather in. The houseboat, the traveling. Letting our children experience the world. Learning from other cultures.

I'm a dreamer, a "go big or go home" kind of girl. I still dream big, and I still want so many of those things that I mentioned above. However, this ladder of success is a slippery slope, and if you aren't careful, you will soon be living your life hustling after the promised land, never satisfied with anything you have in the present, constantly aware of every slightest flaw or broken piece that is keeping you from getting there.

Suddenly, scrolling through Pinterest and pinning your dreams becomes more prominent than laying your life at God's feet. Quickly, everything becomes self-absorbed. This isn't a healthy kind of self-improvement. This self-improvement doesn't look to God for growth—it looks to the left, to the right, and then back at yourself. It's all encompassing, hustling, straining perfecting, constantly looking in the mirror and at yourself and your own dreams, then comparing them to your family's, your friends', and your neighbors' success.

I'd watch my neighbors, friends, and family and all the good things they were doing and immediately raise the bar on my own life.

Oh man, they have only been married for two years and they've already graduated from college, landed awesome jobs, and are building a custom home. What are we doing wrong?

Man, they seem to be traveling all the time and are going on humanitarian trips, plus they are both super fit, skinny, and healthy. Ugh, I'm failing!

I just couldn't seem to work hard enough or fast enough. With every year that passed, every milestone we hit, the demands of perfection got bigger and bigger. And the vice got tighter and tighter. But I kept pushing, kept working. I had been going at this perfectionist thing for so long that I was learning to push through the anxiety, learning to pick myself up faster.

Then we had our first child. And that fear of not being good enough, well, no surprise, it began to bleed into our son's life as well. But it's different with a child.

———

Jakston Paul was born with bright, alive eyes. He's fierce with the most tender heart you could ever have. Jaks is the greatest gift that God has ever given to me. He's still our only child, and thinking about him and the lessons he has taught me, I have no words.

Jaks was named after that same Grandpa Jack that carefully did all he could to get Wes and me together. Grandpa Jack passed away while Wes was serving his mission, and he didn't get to be there when Wes and I got married. Naming our first son after him only seemed fitting.

As a parent, I wanted to give my all to my son. My mom had been the greatest blessing in my life, and I only hoped to give my child the same experience. As parents, we will do anything for our children. We want to give them the ideal environment to thrive in. We never want them to feel "less than" or like they are not enough. We fear not giving them all that they deserve, so we make it our responsibility to do everything perfectly on our end.

I have never felt so much judgment and panic than I did before I had my son. The list of dos and don'ts that we place on each other as parents. It's unreal.

I told myself I will "never do this," and that our child "won't do that." I was determined to teach him how to communicate before he was one. I was thankful I had taken three years of sign language and knew that it would come in handy now. Wes and I had read every book and researched every baby product. We were pretty set on how we wanted to raise Jaks. (I can hear all of the more matured mothers chuckling right now.)

As parents, we subconsciously measure our children against other children, panicking, fearing that if they don't measure up it's our fault. We fear that we will fail as parents.

Since day one, Jaks struggled with sleep. One day, at only two weeks old, he was awake from 8 a.m. until 6 p.m. that night. I had tried every-thing. Literally everything. Wes came home from work, trying to help as well. I'm so thankful I married a man who took an active part in our parenting. We both had no idea what to do.

My mom had stopped by to bring us dinner. I started crying, telling her how embarrassed I was. I couldn't even get my child to sleep! I didn't know what to do. We put Jaks in the car seat and decided to go for a drive. I needed out of the house. Jaks immediately fell asleep, and we drove for two hours. Jaks slept and I cried. I felt like a bad mom. Surely others never had issues like this?

Then there was breastfeeding. Blah. Of course my plan was to breast-feed until my son was twelve months old. I knew that was the "best thing for him." However, that wasn't working well either for a variety of reasons that don't really matter. By four months, I was solely giving Jaks a bottle. I felt like I had failed. That I didn't measure up to "perfect mom" status. I felt judged and insecure.

And the list goes on and on. The demands, expectations, and self-judgment that we inflict on ourselves for not doing things perfectly. Yet I was determined to keep trying, always doing the right thing, keeping up.

———

Just one month after Jaks was born, I went back to work. Sleep had become obsolete. During the day, I would do all I could to be the best mom, conscious of how much TV my child was getting and whether he was learning his ABCs fast enough, monitoring his sugar intake, trying to feed him organic only, making sure we got outside every day.

While he was asleep, I'd quickly go full blast into dream-chasing mode. Working on my business, phone calls with clients. There was no such thing as "downtime." Car rides were meant for catching up on emails, while workouts were for reading the latest self-help book, and vacations were never just vacations.

And of course, every day I tried to do all I could to check off my Christian checklist of scripture reading, personal prayers, family prayers, dinner prayers, family scripture study, service, and church.

It was go, go, go all the time. Every day. After Jaks was born, we decided to move our family to Arizona. It was a clear prompting that Wes and I both knew we needed to follow. We were able to build our first home there. It was modest, but perfect for our new little family of three.

Again, perfect—for a moment. As if being a perfectionist wasn't hard enough, then Pinterest and Instagram were born, making everything seemed flawed and imperfect. Our little house soon became a constant "fixer upper," and we were constantly dreaming of what it would be like when it was "finally the way we loved it." Wes and I would continue to discuss and dream, talking about how "this house is nice" but what we would love in our "next bigger home."

When Jaks was three, I was determined to give him the cutest birthday party ever! It seemed like all my friends were giving their children the cutest themed parties with handouts, elaborate cupcakes, and creative invitations. You know, the works!

I was a graphic designer, so pulling together the perfect invitation, cupcake toppers, and decorations shouldn't have been a problem. It was a superhero party, and I was able to suck in one of my dearest friends to help me. The night before, we stayed up until 1 a.m. making this blue cake on a cake stand. Things weren't working: the frosting had hardened too soon, and we couldn't smooth out the cake. I was feeling stressed and frustrated because it just wouldn't look right.

Finally after surrendering to the point of "good enough," I grabbed the cake to slide it into the fridge, and *wham!* I slammed the cake into the top shelve, and half of it ended up all over my fridge door.

Am I saying that big elaborate birthday parties are bad? No. But the motives and reasons that I chose to do an elaborate party were. For some, this kind of gig is fun and exciting. For me? Not so much. By the time we made it to the party, I was exhausted, and hardly even present. Yet I felt too guilty and worried that I wasn't a good mom if I didn't do it.

And this guilt. It's what I felt, all day, every day.

Guilt for only reading a verse a day in my scriptures.

Guilt for not making enough homemade meals.

Guilt that I fell asleep while praying.

Guilt that my child watched too much TV.

Guilt that I never had enough time for anything that I was doing.

Guilt that I wasn't measuring up.

I had hoped that becoming a wife and a mother would provide the sense of fulfillment I was constantly seeking. But in reality, with each added responsibility, I felt more and more guilt about what I thought I should be. Expectations were higher; responsibilities were growing. It all seemed too much, yet I couldn't see any way out. I was in the heart of a vicious tornado, and the only solution I could think of was to work harder.

FOUR

The Breaking Point

could hear the garage door open. Wes was home. I gathered Jaks and rushed to the door to pass the parent baton off to him. The deadlines that I'd pushed off all day were haunting me. Wes opened the door, and there I stood in the same place I greeted him every day. He looked up at me and I could see it. I tried to brush it off, but it was there. Exhaustion. Heaviness.

"Not today, Tiff."

I went to give him the "you have no idea what I'm up against and all that I have to get done" speech, but I could see his eyes and I held my tongue.

I sat there holding Jaks on my hip, still in my sweats with third-day hair. The kitchen was full of dishes, and I didn't have dinner prepared. I could barely breathe thinking of everything that "still needed to be done." I sat there, motionless, as I watched my husband walk past me and up the stairs. Words weren't needed.

Tears started welling up behind my eyes, and I got a big lump in my throat. *What am I doing? What is this life? Why won't it stop? What am I doing wrong?*

I finished getting Jaks dinner, put his pajamas on, and threw him in the car. Jaks has always been a fighter with sleep. No matter how many times I tried to sleep train him, it didn't work. He has the biggest heart, but he's a fighter, stubborn and independent. We spent so much of his early life traveling that the only place he would easily fall asleep is the car. (Maybe because he was strapped in and would finally hold still long enough to relax.) The days I felt too exhausted to fight him for bed, I would throw him in the car and drive for twenty minutes until he was asleep. Every day was becoming a day of exhaustion, and this habit had become our nightly routine.

It was dark, and I turned on church hymns, hoping Jaks would fall asleep quickly. I needed to get back to work, and I knew tonight was going to be an all-nighter. As I drove around the block, the tears started rolling down my cheeks. I was exhausted. Wes was exhausted. My body hurt, and my heart literally ached. As I drove, a million and one thoughts were racing through my head, and hurt was turning into anger, the same way it did when I couldn't complete a multiplication sheet in third grade.

All I'm trying to do is be good, do good, and make it in this hard world! What does God want from me?! Can't He see that I can't possibly work any harder? Why isn't He giving us a break!?

If I'm being honest, the few months (*year*) up to this point, my spirit had become numb. My prayers were half-hearted. I had gone so long with the same pleading prayers, and I felt like maybe God wasn't listening. Things seemed to be getting worse. The chronic physical pain I was facing each day was increasing, and the mental capacity to keep my mind clear was decreasing. I knew something needed to change, but I didn't understand. What was I doing wrong?

From the outside, it looked like everyone had this whole "successful life" thing figured out—clean houses, smiling faces, service oriented families, involved kids. I tried hard to convince myself that this wasn't true, that there were plenty of others struggling to keep it together, but it didn't help. I felt alone.

The perfect shell I was trying so hard to keep myself in was breaking. My weaknesses and flaws were getting harder and harder to hide—and to be honest, I was tired of hiding them. I was hurting and desperately wished someone would notice.

I looked behind me in the backseat, Jaks was asleep. I slowly rolled into our driveway and waited as the garage door opened.

I could feel myself fading, wanting to wave the white flag. But then there was that voice. That same one that had always been with me.

"You just need to work harder! Work smarter."

This was the only answer and solution that I had ever known: hard work and hustle. And, at the end of the day, it seemed again the only solution I could find.

"Stop making your husband feel so worn out. Start making dinner for your family. You aren't doing enough service. You aren't organized enough. You need to get up early and exercise harder. You aren't keeping your Christian checklist in line, stop missing your scriptures, get to church on time, say more meaningful prayers."

I got Jaks out of the car seat and carried him upstairs to bed. I opened our bedroom door and saw Wes asleep on the bed. I walked downstairs, did the dishes, and then turned my computer back on.

"I just need be more efficient." (As if I hadn't already told myself this a thousand times before.)

I grabbed a notebook and pen and started jotting down all the things I knew I needed to do better. (Again, an exercise I had done a thousand times before.)

- Pick toys up immediately after Jaks is finished playing.
- Load the dishes into the dishwasher immediately after I use them. Stop leaving them in the sink.
- Fold the laundry as it comes out of the dryer.
- Make a grocery list on Sunday and meal prep on Monday.
- Sign up for a triathlon so I stay committed to the gym.
- Listen to my scriptures while I'm driving to the gym.
- Answer emails and texts immediately as they come in. Don't let them get backed up.
- Do more crockpot meals.
- Stop handing Jaks to Wes immediately when he comes home.

The list went on and on (like it always did). I then took out notecards. I wrote fifteen different goals that were lacking in my life and taped them to my wall. I was determined. *I know I can do this. I can keep it together. I just have to work harder.* I stayed up the rest of the night pushing through deadlines, slept an hour, and then went to the gym.

The pain in my body was excruciating, but I pushed it back, trying hard to ignore it. I turned my scriptures on while driving to the gym and then read through emails while I ran on the treadmill.

Once I got home, I continued, trying to utilize every second of time while also being as intentional as I could. To be honest though, my mind was so past exhausted I couldn't feel anything anyway.

I managed to keep up with this schedule. Monday, Tuesday, Wednesday, Thursday. . . . Friday morning, I got in the car to head to the gym and I felt sick. My body hurt. My anxiety felt heavy. I decided to go to the cycle room. There wasn't a class going, and I had the entire place to myself. I jumped on a spin bike and started to pedal. I turned up my music as loud as I could, trying to find motivation.

After twenty minutes, I was feeling extremely fatigued and nauseated. I decided to stop and see if stretching would help. I lifted one leg over my bike to get off. . . .

"No, no, no, NO!"

Extreme pain went shooting through my back, I yelled out and collapsed to the floor. I couldn't breathe. I couldn't move. My back was out. I knew it was bad, and I laid there. Alone.

This can't happen! NO! I have too much to do! I just signed up for a triathlon. I have to get up. I have to keep fighting. But it was useless. I was in too much pain. I tried to play it off, making myself look like I was stretching, just in case someone came in. I started praying. "Please, Heavenly Father, please help me get to my car. Please." I don't know how long I laid there in fetal position, but I know that the only reason I managed to get to the car was because of divine intervention.

I opened the car door and flung my body in awkwardly. The slightest movement sent excruciating pain through my back and down my legs. I grabbed my phone and called Wes. Between laboring breaths I told him what had happened.

"Where are you? Do I need to come get you?"

"No. I'm going to try and drive home."

"Tiff, I'll come get you."

"No. I can do this. It's only a few miles."

I put the key in the ignition and started the car. The pain wouldn't stop. I was holding my breath while trying to keep my foot steady on the gas. If anyone would have seen me, they would have pulled me over for sure. I was half laying down and sideways, doing all I could to keep myself still.

I pulled into the driveway and called Wes.

"Can you please come get me out?"

He walked outside and opened my door. I could tell he was trying to have compassion, but he was fighting frustration and desperation. "Tiff, when will you stop? You can't keep doing this! You have to stop! You have to start listening to your body!"

He carried me to the couch where I crumbled. My body was done. It was fighting against me, pleading for help, and I knew it.

My entire life, I believed that rest, stillness, and slowness were signs of weakness. If you needed rest, you were weak. Inadequate. Not strong enough. If you were slow, you weren't good enough. Even when I felt like I needed a nap, I didn't take one. Saturday morning chores, if I took five minutes resting on the couch—I was lazy. I believed that only the strong made it in this world, and strong is what I needed to be. Our world embeds in us a "survival of the fittest" attitude, and those who are slow, weak, or lazy—they get left behind. The world's voices tell us that only the strongest, fastest, and quickest make it in this world, those that are always one step ahead of the next person.

And this is how I lived, trying with all my might to be strong, to be fine, to have it together. But now? Now I was a fighter who had no more fight to give. All I could do was stay completely still, lying on the couch.

> For a star to be born, there is one thing that must happen: a gaseous nebula must collapse. So collapse. Crumble. This is not your destruction. This is your birth.
>
> —Noor Tagouri[1]

The following week, I couldn't move. As each day passed with no productivity, my to-do lists were piling up. Emails were getting backed up, clients were getting frustrated, neighbors were taking Jaks because I couldn't move from the couch to care for him.

It was frustrating and irritating. I was going numb, and I didn't pray. I didn't read my scriptures. I was angry, at God especially. The good girl inside of me told me I was wrong for being angry at God, but there I lay, unable to move, all for trying so hard to be perfect. So despite what my good girl was telling me, I was angry!

I just needed to keep fighting, keep going, keep pushing. I was afraid to stop, terrified to be still. I tried valiantly to work through it. I'd make it ten minutes on my computer trying to work when my lower back would seize up again and may head would start pounding. My body and mind were fatigued, and trying to be creative just wasn't working.

I'm usually quick to create and quick to move. Not being able to work and do the creative things I loved was humiliating. Nothing was working right, and every attempt to keep my brokenness hidden was comically flimsy. It was becoming obvious to friends, family members, and clients that I was struggling, that I was failing.

I still didn't know what was going on with my body. Sometimes when you are dealing with chronic illness or autoimmune issues, it can take years before you are properly diagnosed. This was the case for me. It took five moves, three states, and too many doctors and tests to count to finally figure out that I was fighting a chronic bladder disease called interstitial cystitis, extreme stage four endometriosis, and an autoimmune disease.

But at this point, we didn't know. Mentally in my mind I had convinced myself that, I must be "making it up." Doctors weren't able to find anything, and it's not like I was bleeding to death or had been in a massive car accident. So trying to tell clients or ward members that you "just don't feel good" (all the time) seemed weak and pathetic. And I didn't want to be weak and pathetic.

Instead of being honest, I tried to cover it up and work through it. I tried to finish jobs and fulfill my church callings while still saying yes to anything that people were asking me to do. Yet it was obvious that I couldn't keep up and that I *wasn't* keeping up. And this only perpetuated the problem. I was committing to things and not performing well, making others upset and frustrated with me.

I remember getting an email from a client telling me "that I wasn't cut out to run a business." Close relatives were telling me "some people just can't handle stress. Maybe you are one of those people."

Comments like this would kill my heart, making me feel yet again "less than." The fighter in me would protest, *But I* am *strong! I am cut out to do all that I'm doing!*

I didn't want to fail. I *couldn't* fail. Yet with everything I was fighting, I *was* failing. Dreams were slipping through my fingers and there was no hiding it. My flaws, cracks, and brokenness were all starting to show. It was literally killing me.

Mentally I was slipping, and physically I was gone. Anxiety and panic attacks were becoming a daily occurrence. I could hardly breathe.

ACCEPT THE HELP AND FIND THE HOPE

I knew I needed help, and I was desperate to figure out how to save my life. I needed advice on how to keep my jumbled mess together. After sharing my fears and anxieties with a dear friend, she suggested that I go see her counselor and mentor. I agreed and called the next week to set up an appointment. I was desperate for help, desperate to save everything that I had worked so hard to build.

Steve has a wise old soul. He's worked with hundreds of people with broken stories and broken hearts. He was and still is an answer to my prayers.

I sat there in my chair wondering what I was going to say when all I could feel was pain, heartache, and turmoil. I looked up and knew that Steve was waiting for me to talk.

"I'm worthless." There was the giant lump in my throat. "I'm worthless, and my life has become a waste."

"Why do you feel that?"

"Everything is falling apart! Everything! Emails are coming in and my clients are upset. I'm missing deadlines. I can't get out of bed. I can't cook or take care of my son. I can't exercise. I'm gaining weight just sitting here. I feel gross, and I just hurt everywhere. We still only have one child—I'm worthless! The last ten years, Wes and I have worked so hard trying to build a life for ourselves, trying to make it in this world and get to a place where we could live our dreams. And now, in a matter of weeks it's crumbling. I can't do anything, and it's affecting every part of our life. I might as well be a bum in LA living on the beach, because right now, we're basically the same!"

"You're right."

I immediately looked up and stared at him.

"You're right. You do have the same amount of worth as that homeless bum in California."

My heart stopped. I wasn't expecting him to agree with me.

"I didn't really mean that. I'm just exhausted, and I don't know what to do."

"No, Tiff. I think you did."

"No, I just meant . . . I mean . . . I know that everyone has worth and that God loves everyone, I didn't mean that, it's just—"

He cut me off. "Tiff, you can't earn your worth."

I stared at him. Trying to think of a million words that could get me out of this. But I couldn't. My stomach dropped.

What was happening? The shock I was experiencing was overwhelming. He was right. I *was* trying to earn my worth. Does God really love us the same?

It was as if someone had blasted a nuclear bomb inside my head. My mind started spiraling. Anger, hurt, all of it was boiling up, and I felt like I was going to explode. My emotions were so heightened that words just started spewing out of my mouth.

I started yelling, "Then what the heck have I been doing for the last fifteen years?! Why have I been trying so dang hard?! So I should have just moved to California and done nothing my entire life?"

I knew that was a completely irrational thing to say, that it wasn't true. But I was furious, not to mention embarrassed, hurt, and confused.

He looked at me. "Everything could fall apart, all of it. It doesn't mean anything. It doesn't mean you're a bad person or that you're a failure. It just means that it fell apart. No judgment needed."

The words stung my heart, and my head was having a hard time wrapping around them. I had lived my entire life knowing that God loves all His children, but in this moment, it was as if I was finally hearing it.

I didn't say much the rest of my session.

Everything felt too much. I couldn't wrap my head around the last fifteen years of my life and how suddenly it all felt in vain. It was as if I was playing *Sorry* and was just about to be home free, when all of a sudden another player wiped all my guys and planted them right back at the beginning.

As I started walking out the door, Steve looked at me.

"Tiff, you're angry at God, and I think you should let Him know that. Stop pretending everything is 'OK and fine'—let Him know how you really feel."

I sort of jerked my head in a half nod and walked out to my car. My heart hurt and I felt numb.

I was on autopilot the rest of the day, the same way I had been for months, going through the motions because I didn't want to feel.

I could hear Steve's words echoing in my mind, *Tell God you're angry at Him.*

To be honest I had stopped praying altogether, at least any heartfelt prayers. I'd maybe kneel down and give a half-said repetitive prayer, but my heart was far away from talking to God. I was angry and I didn't want to admit it. *A good girl is never angry at God, right? And He's God. Of course everything He does is for our good, right?*

I sat there finishing up some last-minute cleaning as I fought the prompting to go talk to God. Jaks and Wes were already asleep for the night. As I walked up to my bedroom, I looked at the bed. Most of me wanted to go to sleep. I didn't want to deal with it. However, God is good even when we are mad at Him, and somehow, I found myself in my closet, kneeling.

I still didn't have words. I didn't know what I was going to say. I was almost too terrified to hear what would come out. I had been stuffing my negative thoughts away for so long that I didn't dare open the door. For thirty minutes, I knelt there in silence before I said anything.

"Heavenly Father . . ."

Those two words were all it took. It was as if an entire dam shattered inside of me and I lost it.

Sobbing, crying, yelling, screaming. Everything was coming out. I told God I was mad at Him. I told Him I was angry. How I didn't understand.

I knew the life I was living wasn't the life He wanted for me, but where was I going wrong? I couldn't be who He wanted me to be. All the lists, the expectations, perfection—I wasn't cut out for it! I couldn't do it, and I didn't know what He wanted me to do, because I was done! For years and years I have tried to do more, be more, yet every single day I was falling short. Keenly aware of everything I wasn't, guilt was my constant companion. Anxiety never left me.

"You said that the gospel of Jesus Christ was supposed to bring me joy, happiness, and peace! Well guess what? I don't feel *any* of those things! Why?! Plus I feel like everyone is angry with me. Clients, friends, family members—I'm failing everyone! And I'm miserable on top of it. I'm sick of it, and I need it to change! Please. Please just make it change."

I sat there sobbing for over thirty more minutes, pouring my heart out to God, until finally, there was nothing left to say. I was exhausted. I lay there, too tired to get up. I cried myself to sleep, and all I remember, right before I drifted off, was a whisper:

"I've missed you, child. I've missed you."

NOTE

1. Noor Tagouri's Facebook page, posted March 16, 2014, accessed June 15, 2017, https://www.facebook.com/ntagouri.

FIVE

Rock Bottom

Something very beautiful happens to people when their world has fallen apart: a humility, a nobility, a higher intelligence emerges at just the point when our knees hit the floor.

—Marianne Williamson[1]

It was two o'clock—*Wes shouldn't be home already*. I sat there looking through the window, confused why I was seeing my husband pulling into the driveway. The door opened, and I immediately saw the weight on his shoulders and the heaviness in his eyes.

I stood there bracing myself. I could tell he didn't have good news.

"They let me go."

Whatever I was holding fell to the floor as I stood there staring at my husband. A million things were running through my head, yet all of it left me motionless.

I walked to my husband and hugged him. There we stood, holding each other, neither of us knowing what to say.

Most often when we pray for aid, we pray having an exact blessing in mind that we want God to give us. When I finally laid everything at God's feet, I prayed for change. In my mind, I wanted that change to be blessings, finances, easier ways, more strength, better health. I wanted more.

God doesn't work the same way we do. I prayed for change, and God heard me. He was anxiously waiting and ready to step in. But not in the way I had hoped. God answered my prayers, but in His way. His answer wasn't more. This time, it was less.

> For my thoughts are not your thoughts, neither are your ways my ways. . . . For as the heavens are higher than the earth, so are my ways higher than your ways, and my thoughts than your thoughts. (Isaiah 55:8–9)

The next few months we were hit with a tsunami of trials. Day by day, things seemed to be cut out of my life. After my back gave out, every other health issue that I had been suppressing shot to the surface, taking all of my responsibilities down with them. I couldn't get out of bed, I couldn't move. I was fighting intense chronic pain, and my insides were turned upside down.

I started going to doctors, trying to find answers. We didn't have insurance, and with the loss of my husband's job, we couldn't afford to get every test done that the doctors were suggesting.

For more than two months, my husband tried looking for work. Submitting his resume to anything and everything he could. Nothing was happening, and we were getting desperate. One day, one of my college best friends called. She had no idea that my husband had lost his job, but she felt prompted to call.

She had recently been informed that a job opening had opened up at the company her husband worked for. We hadn't been in touch for a while, and she said for whatever reason that she had thought about us. Obviously, that "whatever reason" was a direct prompting. The job opening would be a career change for Wes, but it fit everything that he loved and was good at. This was absolutely a blessing. However, the job was in California. And our home was in Arizona.

Due to our circumstance, and thoughtful prayer, we knew we needed to apply for the job. Wes submitted his resume, and the next day they called to see if he could interview. We jumped in the car and drove to California. We were there a total of thirty hours. We drove around the area, Wes interviewed for the job, and then we drove back home.

The next day Wes was offered the job. This was a Friday. By Sunday, we had packed Wes's car up with as many things as we could, and he had left to start work that Monday. I sat in the driveway watching my husband leave. I was thankful for the job. I knew it had been a tender mercy. However, I could barely breathe. I didn't feel good. My body hurt. I loved my home, our neighborhood. I loved Arizona.

And now, the one person who always gave me strength, who always knew what to say, was gone, headed to another state to provide for our family, while I stayed behind trying to get our home up for sale. We couldn't afford two house payments, and we knew until we sold our house that we wouldn't be able to move there together. Our dear friends offered their spare bedroom to Wes until we sold our home. It was extremely humbling for us, but still to this day I am so thankful for their charity and kindness.

When I could no longer see Wes's car, I gathered Jaks in my arms and went inside. I looked around at our home. Memories started flooding my mind. There were a lot of hard times, but it's also where Jaks learned to crawl, to walk. It was where he said his first words. My heart felt like it was going to shatter. All of a sudden, everything about this house seemed perfect. All those nitpicky wants that we used to say we wanted or that we would change in our next home—I couldn't see them. I didn't want to leave.

The next few weeks, my health didn't get any better. Only worse. Exercise became obsolete, taking my mental health with it. I didn't have my husband; I could barely be a mom to the one and only child we had. I had to drop out of the two triathlons that I was signed up for, and now with my health in the state that it was and my husband living in another state, having more children seemed impossible.

In the meantime, I was still trying to manage and run my full-time design and marketing business. Yet with everything that had happened, it was getting harder and harder. I could barely handle getting on the computer at all.

How did everything that felt so right for so long all of a sudden seem so wrong? My fast-paced life was coming to a halting stop. Everything was changing. In a short few weeks the A-to-B road map that I had so carefully sketched out for our family, the one that I had worked so hard to keep up with, was gone. Blown to smithereens.

What was happening? All my years of hard work and hustling—was it all for nothing?! The sleepless nights, the strain, sacrifices, tears . . . was it all in vain? How could God let years and years of hard work go to waste in an instant? Maybe I had never listened to God to begin with?

My business was the last thread I was holding on to, yet I could feel God telling me to walk away from that as well.

I had experienced heartache, pain, and adversity before. I had been through hard hard things. Some still too personal to share. However, for whatever reason, the immensity of these trials happening all at once, they literally shook me to my core.

My physical health was the greatest culprit to this. After years and years of pushing my body past what it could handle, it was done. I was in a lot of pain and completely fatigued. When I physically couldn't do what I needed to do, my mental health spiraled. Day after day, things weren't getting better, and the darkness only got worse. I felt worthless.

The magnitude and speed of the crumbling left me paralyzed. I felt blindsided. I couldn't wrap my head around everything that had transpired in just a short time. It's as if I had walked straight into the belly of my greatest fears. I couldn't seem to find my faith anywhere. Even hope had vanished. I began doubting every prompting I had ever received. I doubted my worth, my past, my future, and my ability to hear God altogether.

Nothing made sense. I was exhausted. Broken. Shattered. Despair consumed me, and I began plummeting into a depression that I had never before experienced.

Some days, the darkness was so heavy that I would text my husband telling him that I wish I wasn't here. That it would be easier to give up, rather than fighting the darkness. To this day I shudder when I think about these moments.

It sounds over the top, but it was real. I'm so thankful that I never went past those few texts to my husband. I never thought about ways to actually take it to the next step. But I know others have.

Depression and anxiety are silent, isolated burdens. You can't physically see if someone is struggling with this kind of anguish. It's not visible. You can't measure it. You can't put it on a chart. It's in our minds. It happens to people who outwardly seem like their life is fine. It happens sometimes for no reason at all.

Mental health is fragile. And truthfully, unless you have experienced a mental illness in some form or another, there is no way for me to describe it without seeming overly dramatic. But it's real. It's real and it's terrifying. I'm not an expert. I don't share this experience because I have all the answers. I share solely because someone, somewhere will read this, and I know they are fighting this battle.

If this is you, if you are that person who is carrying this heavy load, please know that you are loved. That I love you. I wish I could wrap my arms around you right now, right this minute to let you know that you aren't alone. From the bottom of my heart, with ever fiber that I have, keep fighting. We need you. You are important. You have value to add to this world. And you are worth far more than you could ever imagine. I know it seems as though you will never get out of the dark. That the heaviness will last forever. But I promise it won't. I promise! I don't know when that relief is coming. I don't have your answers. But God does. God is aware and He will come! I promise. I'm praying for you. I believe in you.

> The greatest battles of life are fought out daily in the silent chambers of the soul.
>
> —David O. McKay[2]

The darkness I was facing felt as though I had been engulfed by my own raging tempest, pleading, questioning as did the disciples, *"Master, carest thou not that [I] perish?"* (Mark 4:38), or even Job questioning why God had even allowed him to be born. I was sinking, suffocating—everything inside of me was screaming to fight, to keep treading. But I couldn't. I had nothing left.

It took six months for our house to sell. I was excited to finally be with my husband, but leaving Arizona was one of the hardest transitions for me, especially since I wasn't in a good place mentally.

We arrived to pick up our keys with our two U-Hauls, ready to move in. When we got there, the manager of the apartment told us that our apartment wasn't actually ready. When they started to clean the carpets, they realized that it actually needed to be replaced. The previous tenants had been evicted, and they had destroyed the carpet. We had nowhere to go. It would have taken them six more days to finish replacing the carpet, and my parents needed to be back with the U-Hauls in Utah within the next two days. They had no other options for us. We really didn't have any other options either. So they gave us our keys, and we took it as it was.

I'm not sure why this happens, but when you are in such a bad place mentally, every little bump in the road becomes magnified. If you aren't careful, you soon become a magnet for all negativity in general. I was trying so hard to have a positive attitude about it, yet there I was, hauling box after box into our new apartment that was less than half the size of the house we left in Arizona. It was dark and had carpet that I couldn't let my three-year-old walk on without shoes.

Again, it's perspective, right? There are plenty of people in this world who would have opened their arms gratefully to that apartment. And I was grateful to be with my husband, and to be together as a family again, and that he had a job. But I was experiencing such extreme anxiety, and everything felt overwhelming.

My parents stayed as long as they could. But they had to be home for prior engagements two days after we got there. While my mom frantically unboxed everything she could and my dad and husband put together beds and furniture, I sat on the floor, staring at everything that needed to be done.

When my parents left, I could see the panic in their eyes. They knew they weren't leaving me in good condition, and it was breaking their hearts. I tried telling them I would be OK, that I was already OK. But we all knew I wasn't. I wasn't OK. I didn't know how to be OK, or how to even function.

I walked back into the house holding Jaks. Wes had left for work. Boxes were still everywhere, piled high. I didn't know where to put anything. I was in a new place, new environment. I could hear the neighbors yelling at each other, doors slamming, people walking above me. Jaks was trying to dig through boxes to find his toys. He kept telling me he missed our old house and wanted to go back to his friends. I did too.

For the next few months, I sat. Most days you would find me in my husband's sweats with a big T-shirt, lying in bed. Some mornings, I would attempt to get out of bed. I'd walk to the kitchen, stand there, get overwhelmed by the thought of even making breakfast, then I'd grab a granola bar for Jaks and walk back to bed.

I was fighting chronic daily pain, and it was altering every part of my life. My son started accepting that most days included Netflix and any new iPad game he wanted. I never cleaned, and if Wes wanted a home-cooked meal, he cooked it himself.

One day, my sister-in-law was watching Jaks. He was only three. He went running across her kitchen floor, only to stop, look up, and proclaim, "I love your house! Our floors have dried up guacamole all over them!"

He didn't know any different. Just stating the facts. A couple weeks later I had found enough enthusiasm that I got dressed. Meaning, I was able to get myself out of my husband's sweats and large T-shirt and into leggings and a cardigan. I was putting on my shoes when Jaks came into my room, looked at me, and said, "Mom! Why are we going to church?" He wasn't used to me changing out of my sweats. Or even putting shoes on for the day.

Days that were once filled with hustling after my dreams, taking my child on outings, making healthy dinners, working through the nights and putting together extravagant holidays were now replaced with days lying in bed, my child playing on the iPad all day, no work, no exercise, and a husband who brought home pizza every night or ate microwave meals for dinner.

Everything that I ever was, or had been, was no longer there. I was a college athlete who couldn't even walk around the block. I was a creative graphic designer and business owner who couldn't find enough light to do anything creative. I was a good mom who constantly took my son on out-ings, while capturing the happy moments of our day—and now I was the mom with only one child and who couldn't get up long enough to even make her child breakfast. Everything, that I ever thought I was, or that I had prided myself in being, was gone!

The scripture "be still and know that I am God" was the only thread that I could hold on to. Over and over I would try and say this scripture in my mind. And the only prayer I could offer was a quiet plea telling God that I had lost my fight. That I surrendered. Henry B. Eyring said that "acting on even a twig of faith allows God to grow it."[3] I'm not sure my faith was even the size of a twig, but I testify that it was enough.

DESPERATE FOR ANSWERS

Something needed to change. I was miserable. It was hell. I remem-ber dragging myself to church one Sunday, and when the opening song started, the flood gates opened. Tears streamed down my face. I couldn't stop. I couldn't breathe. The heartache was too much. I immediately stood up and fled to my car, where I sobbed uncontrollably. The anxiety was more than I could handle, and the worthlessness I felt was unbear-able. I was miserable, broken, shattered. The questions and doubt that flooded my mind were paralyzing. Who was I if I wasn't everything that I did? How could I possibly have worth while sitting in bed, day after day? What had I done wrong? Where did I go wrong? All I had ever tried to do was be good and do good. I was a good person. Why was everything crumbling? Where did I fit in? What if we never had more children?

I had been taught my entire life that being a member of the Church of Jesus Christ of Latter-day Saints meant that I should be one of the happiest people on earth. That I should be joyful, full of peace. Yet it seemed as though the feelings I felt most were stress, guilt, and anxiety for everything that I wasn't. What was I doing wrong? I knew I was supposed to be perfect like Christ, but how could I possibly try any harder? I was still so far from perfection, and now I had nothing left to give. How could I ever have hope when I felt like I was failing every single day?

I had a testimony that my Savior's Atonement was real, I believed His miracles, I believed Him when He said that "all things are possible to him that believeth" (Mark 9:23)—but in my most broken state, I wasn't sure how to use His power. I knew how to use the Savior's Atonement for repentance, but how did I use Him to heal my shattered mind? How did I use the Savior's power and grace? How could Christ raise me from this state of worthlessness that I felt?

I needed answers in a way I never had before. The answers I needed were far greater than "where should I go to college" or even "who should I marry." I needed to know that I was a daughter of God. I needed to know my worth. I needed to know that my heartache had purpose. I needed to know that there was hope, that this too really would pass. I needed to know that the Atonement could indeed heal my broken heart and mind. I needed to know if everything I had ever believed in was actually true.

And more than knowing, I needed to *feel*. I needed to feel that there is power that exists in being a daughter of God. I needed to feel the healing that only Christ's Atonement could bring. I needed to know firsthand that I, Tiffany Webster, was indeed "graven . . . upon the palms of [His] hands" (Isaiah 49:16), and that Christ had not forsaken me.

In my darkest hour, I knew I had two choices. I could stay in the mental anguish and hell that I was experiencing, or I could choose to fight. I could choose to put God's promises to the test in a way I never had before.

> Ask, and it shall be given unto you; seek, and ye shall find; knock, and it shall be opened unto you. (3 Nephi 14:7)

So I asked. And I did seek. And I knocked in a way I never had before.

With nowhere else to go and nothing else to do, I opened my scriptures—not to check something off my Christian checklist, but to find answers. To find hope. To find my Savior.

NOTES

1. Marianne Williamson's Facebook page, posted August 31, 2013, accessed June 15, 2017, https://www.facebook.com/pg/williamsonmarianne.
2. David O. McKay, in Conference Report, October 1954, 82; see also Brigham Clegg, "Speakers' Contest: 'Sacrifice,'" *Improvement Era* 5, no. 9 (July 1902): 684.
3. Henry B. Eyring, "Mountains to Climb," *Ensign*, May 2012, 24.

PART TWO

Set Free

SIX

Broken Things to Mend

Когда the Apostles left to go to the other side of Bethsaida, they left
Jesus Christ behind so He could be alone. Jesus had received the
news that John the Baptist, His beloved friend and cousin, had been
beheaded by Herod, and after feeding a multitude of people, Jesus was
desperately trying to find solitude.

The disciples took a ship and headed out for the night. Soon after
that, the disciples found themselves in a terrible storm. "But the ship was
now in the midst of the sea, tossed with waves: for the wind was con-
trary" (Matthew 14:24). Unlike the first time the disciples were drown-
ing in a tempest on the sea, Christ wasn't with them—they were alone.
After enduring the wind and waves for most the night, the disciples saw
a figure walking toward them, adding more fear to an already terrifying
experience.

> And in the fourth watch of the night Jesus went unto them, walking
> on the sea.
> And when the disciples saw him walking on the sea, they are
> troubled, saying, It is a spirit; and they cried out for fear. (Matthew
> 14: 25–26)

These experienced sailors and fishermen had endured many storms,
but nothing had prepared them for seeing a figure walking toward
them on a stormy sea. What reason would they have to suspect that this

frightening figure was actually their Savior? To their knowledge, Jesus was back on shore, unaware of His disciples' plight. They didn't expect Him to rescue them. Yet this terrifying spirit *was* their Savior coming to rescue them.

> Be of good cheer; it is I; be not afraid. (Matthew 14:27)

This "fearful being" not only was their Lord and Savior but this terrifying experience also became one of the greatest miracles and blessings that the disciples would ever witness. How often do we mistake the Lord's saving hand as frightening and terrifying?

When my life seemed to fall apart, I in no way would have ever believed that it was God's hand stepping in to save me. I especially wouldn't have guessed that each one of these "fearful" experiences was preparing me for my life's greatest miracles. Wes losing his job, moving away from our home, closing my business, dealing with infertility, struggling with chronic health issues—each of these events has had me crying out in fear, "Master, carest thou not that [I] perish?" (Mark 4:38). My limited perspective felt as though these experiences were destroying me. Yet they were God's way of sending help, His way of sending Christ to save, change, and free me.

I had feared stillness my entire life. I feared that if I stayed put, sat, or took time to rest, that I would fall behind. As a perfectionist, my mind was never still. Loud noises, voices, guilt, and stress constantly occupied my mind. Moving kept me going. When I was moving, I felt like I was progressing.

What I didn't realize was that moving at such a fast pace all the time had actually cost me a great deal. Sure, movement may have made me feel like I was progressing toward my dreams and goals. However, constant movement was also costing me the companionship of the Spirit. Constant movement, physical and mental, was making it harder and harder to feel and hear the Holy Ghost.

When this would happen, I would try to do more. I noticed that I couldn't hear the Spirit very well, so I would read more scriptures and say more fervent prayers. I would beat myself up for not doing enough on my Christian checklist. These "failures" made me believe that I wasn't worthy enough for the Spirit to be with me or that I wasn't doing enough to earn it. How could the Spirit even talk to me if I wanted it to? Sure, I was proactively doing more, but I never gave the Spirit a chance to do its part. My prayers were always flooded with asking and pleading, but rarely ever listening. I was so fatigued that even when I was still, I was half asleep because my body was exhausted. I was using my very best self for the world, and my spiritual needs were getting the most exhausted and fatigued part of my day.

The Holy Ghost is a *still* small voice, a voice that can't be heard when our life is maxed to the limit. I didn't realize that finding stillness in my outward life would become vital to the stillness I needed inside to communicate with God on an entirely different level.

> It was not a voice of thunder, neither was it a voice of a great tumultuous noise, but behold, it was a still voice of perfect mildness, as if it had been a whisper. (Helaman 5:30)

The terrifying experience of forced stillness was the greatest blessing I never knew to ask for. Forced stillness made me stop and listen. All of a sudden I was teachable. I was open and available to hear God's voice.

LEARNING TO BE STILL

It was pizza night for my boys. I was still sick fighting chronic pain and eating out had become a normal occurrence.

Wes got home and I hopped in the car; it was the first time in a few days I had left our apartment. I walked in to order our usual Hot-N-Ready cheese pizza.

"Sorry, ma'am. We've run out and they won't be ready for fifteen minutes."

I wasn't in a rush, and it felt good to be out of the house.

"That's fine. I'll wait here."

I sat in a chair and looked out the windows. Usually, I would have taken that down moment to dig into my phone and check emails, work, or scroll through social media. But I no longer had a business to run, and I had left my phone in the car. Less than two minutes after I walked in, two other women came rushing through the door to order as well. I'm naturally a people watcher, and without my phone, I just sat there completely present in the moment. I'm not sure why, but I could feel God's presence and everything instantly moved in slow motion. I watched as each of these women went to the counter to order pizza, only to receive the same news that I had. Instantly, both of these women became flustered, panicked, and frantic. "What do you mean you don't have a Hot-N-Ready ready?"

Both of them then stormed out in a rush, declaring that they didn't have fifteen minutes to wait for the next batch. I sat in awe as they ran to their cars, jumped in, and drove away. My heart sank, and I widened my eyes in shock. I can't really explain what happened in that moment. It was as if God was giving me my own *Christmas Carol* experience. I was Scrooge being shown my past. Months earlier, I would have been oblivious to what had happened. I would have been sunk in my phone, or I too would have mostly likely stormed out in a rush, frantically driving to the next fastest option.

I felt like the breath had been knocked out of me. What had happened to my life that I didn't even have fifteen minutes to wait for a pizza? That wasn't a life. That wasn't living. My entire life was going past me, and I was in a frantic state completely bypassing life altogether. What had happened? How was that living? It wasn't. I wasn't living. I was storming through life on a fast-paced track, desperately hoping that maybe I'd finally arrive to a place that was still, a place where I was content. Maybe after we got in our dream home and Wes got that big promotion, maybe when my business was streamlined and we had residual income, maybe, maybe, maybe. But *when?*

That promised land I thought I was someday going to get to didn't exist. It never did. It was a mirage planted by the adversary to keep me running. Running in a dry, empty desert to something that wasn't real. My eyes welled up and I sat there, waiting for my pizza and pleading to God, "I don't want to live like that anymore, God. I want something more. I want something better."

It was the very first flicker of light that I had felt in months, and I saw that maybe there was more to these trials than heartache. Maybe God allowed these stumbling blocks to happen, because it was the only way I would listen. Maybe God truly had a better way.

It didn't feel like a miracle at the moment, only a slight shift. Yet now I can see that it was much more than a shift; it was a miracle. I was given a flicker of hope. Hope that God really did have purpose in my trials and a purpose for me. Hope that maybe there was a better way to live. And hope that there was a different life, one that could give me happiness and joy.

For weeks, I had pleaded with God to help me feel better and to make my trials go away. I was reading different verses of scripture, hoping to earn blessings. I had been hoping to earn my health back. I thought I wanted things to go back to how they were. I thought I wanted my health back so I could get back to chasing my dreams and get back on track. In that moment, I didn't want my old life back. I didn't want to be stressed, anxious, and maxed out all the time. I wanted a life where I had fifteen extra minutes to wait for a cheese pizza, a life where I wasn't rushed, but at peace, where I actually felt enough.

The next morning I woke up and pled for God's help.

"Please, Heavenly Father, where was I going wrong? I still feel incredibly worthless. I can't seem to find reason or purpose to try again. How can I fulfill everything that is required of me to be successful, but still live? How can I live a life where I feel enough? How can I have peace, and happiness? Why do I always feel like a failure? How do I find joy again? How can I use Christ's Atonement to heal me?"

I opened my scriptures. I knew the answers lay inside those pages, but to be honest, I didn't know how to find them. Out of habit, I opened up my Book of Mormon to 1 Nephi.

> I, Nephi, having been born of goodly parents, therefore I was taught somewhat in all the learning of my father . . . (1 Nephi 1:1)

My mind immediately started to numb out. Now, I know these verses are important. Nephi is one of my top five people I want to meet when I die. He's amazing. His story is incredible and powerful. However, I had read those words so many times on autopilot that reading them again put me straight back into cruise control. I was reading out of duty, not for help. Albert Einstein is credited with saying that "insanity is doing the same thing over and over again and expecting different results."

Reading the scriptures blesses our lives no matter the effort, but I needed more! I needed help and answers. I needed the scriptures to teach me in a way they never had before. I said another prayer asking that God would help me keep trying, even though all I wanted to do was numb out with another Netflix show.

I decided to grab my iPad and open my Gospel Library app. I wasn't sure what I was going to do, but I started opening conference talks and scrolling through them. After what seemed like an hour of scrolling through talks, I found myself staring at one. I could hear God whisper, "Read this."

"Broken Things to Mend" by Jeffrey R. Holland.

I hesitated. I loved the talk, but I had read it numerous times. Jeffrey R. Holland is my hero, and this talk spoke to me the first time he gave it.

Its beautiful insight about mental illness was inspiring and comforting. Yet I felt hesitant to read it because with so many options out there, why would God lead me to the same talk I've already read multiple times?

"Open the talk, Tiffany."

I could feel the Spirit asking me if I wanted God to teach me or not. Humbled, I opened the talk and with a mighty prayer in my heart I pleaded that God would teach me something new, that He would open my eyes. I began reading.

> I speak to those who are facing personal trials and family struggles, those who endure conflicts fought in the lonely foxholes of the heart, those trying to hold back floodwaters of despair that sometimes wash over us like a tsunami of the soul. I wish to speak particularly to you who feel your lives are broken, seemingly beyond repair.[1]

I thought the first time I read this I could relate to those words. But never before had I felt so broken and conflicted in the lonely foxhole of my heart. The words pierced my heart.

> To all such I offer the surest and sweetest remedy that I know. It is found in the clarion call the Savior of the world Himself gave. He said it in the beginning of His ministry, and He said it in the end. He said it to believers, and He said it to those who were not so sure. He said to everyone, whatever their personal problems might be:
>
> "Come unto me, all ye that labour and are heavy laden, and I will give you rest.
>
> "Take my yoke upon you, and learn of me; for I am meek and lowly in heart: and ye shall find rest unto your souls." (Matthew 11: 28–19)[2]

There it was again. That same answer I had heard so many times in my life. "Come unto Me." What was I missing? Nothing in my life felt restful. I was heavy; I was weak. I knew I was falling short with all my Christian priorities. But why was it all so hard? Why did it feel like the harder I tried to be like Christ, the greater my anxiety became?

I continued to read. The words were different this time. Or maybe I was different. I was desperate, pleading.

And then it happened. My heart and mind were opened.

> It seems clear that the essence of our duty and the fundamental requirement of our mortal life is captured in these brief phrases ["Come unto Me"] from any number of scenes in the Savior's mortal ministry.

He is saying to us, "Trust me, learn of me, do what I do. Then, when you walk where *I* am going," He says, "we can talk about where *you* are going, and the problems you face and the troubles you have . . ."[3]

When Joseph Smith was in desperate need of answers to know which church to join, he fled to the scriptures. He was confused, conflicted, and in turmoil. I could not eloquently portray any better than Joseph Smith did when he described what transpired while he read the famous and beloved version of James 1:5.

> Never did any passage of scripture come with more power to the heart of man than this did at this time to mine. It seemed to enter with great force into every feeling of my heart. I reflected on it again and again, knowing that if any person needed wisdom from God, I did; for how to act I did not know. (Joseph Smith—History 1:12)

My entire life all I wanted to do was be good like my Savior, Jesus Christ. I wanted to live by Christian standards and be known for my kindness, service, and love. I thought I had been moving in the right direction, but really I was slowly drifting away, I had become so trapped by the checklist of perfection and the demands of the world that I lost Christ.

The words echoed into my heart and mind again, and again.

> When you walk where I am going . . . we can talk about where you are going, and the problems you face and the troubles you have.[4]

I could hear God's voice.

"Tiffany. You have been worrying too much about where *you* are going. What *you* are doing. And who *you* are becoming. You have lost my Son. You have lost your Brother. You have spent too much time trying to be like Him that you don't even know who He is."

My heart started pounding. I couldn't breathe. Guilt washed over me like molten lava. *What have I done?*

"My daughter. I have allowed you to come here, because you wouldn't listen. You wouldn't stop. Your life was bound by a vice of perfection and I was losing you. I was losing you."

> No matter how hard we work, no matter how much we obey, no matter how many good things we do in this life, it would not be enough were it not for Jesus Christ and His loving grace. On our own we cannot earn the kingdom of God, no matter what we do. Unfortunately, there

are some within the Church who have become so preoccupied with performing good works that they forget that those works—as good as they may be—are hollow unless they are accompanied by a complete dependence on Christ.

—M. Russell Ballard[5]

IS YOUR MODERN-DAY CHECKLIST KEEPING YOU FROM KNOWING CHRIST?

As I came to a realization of how far I'd drifted from actually knowing my Savior, I saw myself as the Jews who lived at the time of Jesus. At that time, the Jews were living the law of Moses.

This law that was first given to Moses to aid in helping the children of Israel remember that God had transformed into being the law that governed everything that the Jews did. By the time Jesus Christ was born, the Jewish people were being governed by over six hundred laws and prohibitions.

When Moses first received the law, the Israelites were in a state of rebellion against God. The purpose of the commandments and laws were to help the Israelites remember who God was and all that He had done for them.

> And now I say unto you that it was expedient that there should be a law given to the children of Israel, yea, even a very strict law; for they were a stiffnecked people, quick to do iniquity, and slow to remember the Lord their God;
>
> Therefore there was a law given them, yea, a law of performances and of ordinances, a law which they were to observe strictly from day to day, to keep them in remembrance of God and their duty towards him. (Mosiah 13:29–30)

Unfortunately, thanks to that evil cunning one, the people soon became overly obsessed with the law. Over generations, the purpose of the commandments no longer served in helping God's children remember Him, but they became a literal list and protocol of what was required of them to enter Heaven. Only by living in perfect obedience to these laws could you earn your salvation.

Centuries of reverence for the Law as the revelation of God to Moses had created an almost fanatical devotion to its precepts in the hearts and minds of most Jews. Thus, the Law of Moses was no longer perceived in Jesus' day as an expression of God's will; rather, for Jews the Law of Moses had gradually become identified as the divine will itself—perfect, absolute, forever unchanging and unchangeable. The Law was thought of as the will of God exactly, precisely expressed; therefore, any deviation at all from the letter of the Law of Moses was also deviation from God. There was no room for flexibility or "extenuating circumstances."

—Stephen E. Robinson[6]

With every generation that passed, this mentality and belief grew. By the time our Savior came to the earth, the Jews were so keenly focused on "earning" their salvation, that they completely dismissed Jesus Christ. They didn't know who He was and denied their desperate need for a Savior.

How devastating this must have been for Christ, knowing that His own people, those who were supposed to worship Him as their Lord ended up being the very souls who would kill Him. Now, I know this was the case for a select group of Jews. They were so intensely removed from light and truth that they were outraged at the truths and new law that Christ was trying to bring to the earth. However, I can't help but feel that for the rest of the Jews, they were simply too caught up in the ways of their fathers to even notice that Christ was alive. To them, they were doing what they had been taught to earn salvation. Their fathers lived the law of Moses, and their grandfathers lived the law of Moses, carefully judging every law that they were or weren't living—counting steps, looking right, looking left, measuring their success and obedience against their neighbors, friends, and family, judging those around them, while harshly judging their own progress as well. All while Jesus came, lived, and died for them.

It's interesting, isn't it? Thousands of years later, a time when Jesus Christ is about to reign on this earth again, Satan would use the same tactic. Satan may be deceivingly wise, but he isn't that creative. If distracting the Jews from truth worked the first time, why would He do something different? Today as followers of the gospel of Jesus Christ, we are His people. The ones chosen to honor Him and accept Him as our King for the second and final time that He comes to this earth.

And here we are again, consumed with "laws," consumed with Christian and worldly checklists and long to-do lists. Loud voices tell us to be this and to do that, and we listen. We keep our eyes fastened to our left and right, comparing our success to how well our neighbors, friends, and family are checking off their lists. Satan keeps us distracted, while slowly drawing our hearts away from Christ.

I couldn't believe it. I had tried desperately to be good my entire life, tried not to make mistakes, yet there I was, completely removed from Christ. I knelt in prayer and prayed with the most sincere, humbled heart I had ever had. I wasn't angry—I knew I had been wrong. I pled for forgiveness for being so caught up in what others thought of me, of what I thought of myself. I then prayed for direction and asked where to begin.

> Those who have a broken heart and a contrite spirit are willing to do anything and everything that God asks of them.
>
> —Bruce D. Porter[7]

If there was ever a time in my life that I had a contrite spirit and broken heart, it was that day. I made a decision: I was going to let my entire checklist fall to the wayside for a while, all the demands and expectations, gone. Except one.

TO-DO LIST

Know Jesus

NOTES

1. Jeffrey R. Holland, "Broken Things to Mend," *Ensign*, May 2006.
2. Ibid.
3. Ibid.
4. Ibid.
5. M. Russell Ballard, "Building Bridges of Understanding," *Ensign*, June 1998.
6. Stephen E. Robinson, "The Law after Christ," *Ensign*, September 1983.
7. Bruce D. Porter, "A Broken Heart and a Contrite Spirit," *Ensign*, November 2007, 32.

SEVEN

The Perfect Lie

When you need answers to questions that have eternal impact on your life—questions about God, Jesus Christ, the gospel, or your divine worth—you have to fight for them. Scratch that. You *will* fight for them. Acquiring eternal truth means going to war.

Why? Because when you are fighting for truth, you are at war with the one being who will do anything in his power to stop you from knowing. You are up against the one who was a murderer from the beginning. The father, founder, and author of *all* lies.

> [Satan] was a murderer from the beginning, and abode not in the truth, because there is no truth in him. When he speaketh a lie, he speaketh of his own: for he is a liar, and the father of it. (John 8:44)

> And he became Satan, yea, even the devil, the father of all lies, to deceive and to blind men, and to lead them captive at his will. (Moses 4:4)

Why would he care so much about you finding truth? It's simple: the truth will set you free.

> Ye shall know the truth, and the truth shall make you free. (John 8:32)

Freedom is the last thing that Satan would ever want you to have. He is in a prison of damnation, and that is his future. There is no hope for him—no choice, no progression. The only thing he can do now is imprison as many of God's children as he can. Holding God's children captive brings him satisfaction. It is his quest, and he won't stop until the day that he is forever bound by God.

I don't share this to discourage anyone. I also don't share this lightly. I know how serious it sounds. It is serious. I don't share this to make anyone feel like there isn't hope, because this story ends with the brightest of hope and joy! This story ends with freedom! I share this because it needs to be said. Finding truth isn't an overnight experience. Finding truth takes work. It takes one-on-one mentoring with God and His words. It takes diligence, persistence, commitment, and time.

But I testify that truth is ours. God's promises are real. When He said "if any of you lack wisdom" (James 1:5), He wasn't talking about the other guy. He wasn't talking solely about prophets. He wasn't just talking about me. He said "any of you": you, me, or even the greatest of sinners. God's truth is available to all, and so is His freedom!

No, God didn't pull me out of the bottom depths of the sea and onto the highest mountain in one day, or even in one month for that matter. But He took my hand, and that was enough.

UNRAVELING THE LIE

Today the modern dictionary defines perfection as a condition, state, or quality that is free from flaws or defects. As a verb, it is defined as the action or process of improving something until it is faultless.

This goal of perfection seeps into every aspect of the world—businesses, products, commercials, marketing campaigns—each trying to outdo the next best thing, researching, nitpicking, analyzing, judging even the slightest crack or flaw in the system. Magazine companies Photoshop images until every last pixel is perfect. Instagram feeds are being curated to look perfectly, naturally, in sync and flawless.

Perfectionism bombards us at every corner, and the intense competition to be better than the next guy is growing at an increasingly rapid rate. The most elite college program requires you to have higher than a 4.0 (better than perfection). Athletics has become so competitive that unless you start a sport at the age of three, you might as well forget about playing altogether.

And this is what perfectionism does. It cultivates an all-or-nothing approach to everything we do. As a perfectionist, you are given two options: to be perfect, or to fail.

When my race car wasn't moving years ago on the multiplication racetrack, it wasn't enough for me to just get on the track. No, to feel like I had succeeded, I needed to be first, the best. I needed to make it to the fastest time.

During the softball game as a freshman in high school, it didn't matter that we were winning as a team, or that I had ten strikeouts in the game. In my mind, because I walked four people in a row, I had failed.

As years went by, this measurement of success and failure became a regular occurrence. If I wasn't the best, I had failed. If I wasn't perfect, I wasn't enough. The desire to be the best consumed me. Not because I hated the people who were better than me or that I held some undeserved grudge against them, but because I felt like I wasn't enough if someone else was succeeding more than I was. And I hated that feeling of not measuring up. I feared that feeling. So I did all I could to prove to myself that I *was* enough.

PERFECTIONISM VS. BEING PERFECTED

Who do you think curated this definition of perfection for these latter days?

Yep. The author of lies. Why? Well, because the quest for perfection can become prime feeding ground for even the most innocent of souls, and he knows that!

If Satan could redefine the world's definition of perfection, he could then bleed this definition into "God's word," thus changing the perception of "God's truth."

And he did. And it became the Perfect Lie.

Satan laid the Perfect Lie at my feet, and I believed it. Why wouldn't I? God's words tell us "Be ye therefore perfect, even your Father which is in heaven is perfect" (Matthew 5:48). So being exactly like Christ is what I was determined to do. And with the "Choose the Right" shield imprinted on my heart and my "What Would Jesus Do" bracelet on my wrist, I took that Perfect Lie lure, and I ate it right up. My favorite primary song was "I'm Trying to Be Like Jesus," and that truth became the core of everything that led me.

Now, don't get me wrong. Becoming like Christ *is* the ultimate goal, and we absolutely need to try and do as Jesus would do, but berating ourselves for every mistake we make is no way to get there. Jesus Christ has power to change us. When we fill our minds with discouragement that we will never be enough, we are discounting who Jesus Christ actually is. When we think we are too broken to save, we are essentially saying that Christ doesn't have the power to heal every wound. If we believe we are irreparable, we don't believe that Christ is who He says He is. Self-deprecation and belittlement are Satan's ways of making us lose hope: hope that we can change and hope that we don't have to do it alone. It was such a shock to me when I realized that self-deprecation is actually pride.

In my mind, if Christ is what I needed to be equal to, then I need to continually be aware of where I was lacking and what I needed to do to get there. I believed I constantly needed to be more, do more, and have more so that I could be "just like Christ."

In other words, Satan had me believing that I needed to live my life by this equation:

THE PERFECT LIE

Me + More = Christ

Every day, I would measure myself against this equation. Beating myself up for how far I'd fall short. Ending the night discouraged by how much more I needed to do and become before I would be enough.

"Christ would have said that differently." (*Beat myself up.*) "Christ would have done His visiting teaching and taken meals to the two ladies who just had babies." (*Ugh.*) "Christ would be able to forgive that person's actions; why are you still thinking about it? Let it go!" (*You are such a screw up, you'll never get there!*)

Then I would think about the two options I had again: I could keep trying and carry the chains of constant failure, or I could abandon the quest and leave my faith. Leaving was still never an option. So trying harder is what I did. It's all I believed I could do.

I need to be more forgiving. More charitable. Have more humility. Say more fervent prayers. Be more patient. Do more service. Take more meals to my neighbors. Show more kindness. Be more understanding, less judgmental. Have more strength.

Me + More Forgiveness = Christlike
Me + More Charity = Christlike
Me + More Prayerful = Christlike
Me + More Patient = Christlike
Me + More Service = Christlike
Me + More Meals to my Neighbor = Christlike

More. More. More.

It was exhausting. This quest to be "just like Christ"—it's like being on a hunt for the gold treasure, but your map seems to be taking you in circles. And so you walk, and walk, and walk, getting *nowhere*. It's maddening.

And that's why it's the Perfect Lie. Because it's a fraud! Let's really look at this equation carefully. Christ is the Only Begotten Son. The *only* person to ever walk this earth "perfectly." He is the *only* person who could become the Savior of the world. He was born half mortal and half God. He was born perfect, and He stayed perfect! He was the only person to pass through this life sinless.

Even if we were to walk perfectly and be flawless in all that we did, could we ever in this mortal life be "just like Christ"? What could we possibly add upon ourselves that would make this equation complete?

Me + _____ = Christ

Nothing! Absolutely, 100 percent, *nothing*! You could perform a million, perfect flawless actions, and you would still fall short of being "equal" to Christ.

Jesus Christ *is* Jesus Christ. He is the Son of God, the Redeemer of the World, Lord of Lords, King of Kings, Alpha and Omega, the Beginning and the End, the Light of the World. How could anything we do—no matter how hard we try, or how little we sleep—how will it ever become equal to Jesus Christ, the one infinite being, who atoned intimately for each and every person that walked this earth?

It can't.

It's an impossible math equation. It sets us up for failure. Every. Single. Day. Making it the Perfect Lie: the Perfect Lie to keep Christians like you and me discouraged, hopeless, and mad.

(Blah! I want to scream).

But of course it doesn't stop there. If the Perfect Lie isn't destructive enough, Satan takes us one step deeper, maybe even further than that.

THE PERFECT LIE REMOVES US FROM CHRIST ALTOGETHER. ONCE SATAN HAS US HOPELESSLY TRYING TO BE LIKE CHRIST, HE THEN REMOVES CHRIST FROM THE EQUATION COMPLETELY.

Once we are on autopilot, trying with all our might to check off our "Christian to-dos"—Satan then whispers these alternatives into our ears, alternate equations that he promises will make us happy, satisfied, and content. One of these equations that wreaked havoc in my life was this:

Me + Skinnier Body = Happy

And others will he pacify, and lull them away into carnal security, that they will say: All is well . . . and thus the devil cheateth their souls, and leadeth them away carefully down to hell. (2 Nephi 28:21)

Up until the last few years, my body and I have always had a love/hate relationship—minus the love. I have always been convinced that my body was the one thing that kept me away from being happy.

As a child, I had a heightened sensitivity to my body. I knew that mine was bigger than my friends'. I was aware that I was taller than all the boys.

Through my teenage years, I was sure my body was the thing that would keep me away from finding someone who would love me. I didn't think I was pretty. I spent more time crying in the mirror than I care to admit. The few dances I went to in high school always began with a complete breakdown of tears while getting ready, questioning if I should even go to the dance at all, wanting and wishing so badly that I could feel beautiful. I saw girls who seemed to look good in everything they wore. I dreamt of being like that, of feeling that way.

When I got married, I still hated my body. It didn't matter how often Wes told me that he loved me and that he loved my body the way it was. I couldn't accept it. I exercised and exercised, dieted and dieted. But I was always ten to fifteen pounds and two jean sizes away from being happy.

It's an exhausting yo-yo ride, berating your body, looking at it with disgust, embarrassed at every little flaw it has.

Food was the enemy and my body the victim. It was the one thing that held me back! If I could just get it controlled and right where I want it—I could finally be happy. It consumed my life. I didn't wake up thinking about Christ; I woke up thinking about working out and what I was or wasn't going to eat that day.

Somehow I had time to read the latest food trends and weight-loss books. I had time to pin the quickest and most efficient workouts. But I barely had time to read my scriptures? It's a slippery slope. I didn't realize it at the time, but this alternative equation to be fit and skinny—it had become a bigger priority than my relationship with Jesus. And slowly, Christ had completely been removed from the forefront of my mind altogether.

Like all of Satan's tactics, these equations come in all shapes and sizes, depending on what we feel we need to be in order to feel enough. We each have different needs, different seasons. Some of us believe when we have enough money we will be happy and feel successful. As teenagers, we believe marriage is the key to our happiness. We think when we graduate college we can start living. If we have more social media followers, we'll be accepted. When our houses are decorated, then they will feel like homes.

Me + Skinnier = Loved
Me + Prettier = Accepted
Me + Athletic = Fit In
Me + Outgoing = Friends
Me + Married = Happy
Me + Money = Successful

Suddenly, these alternative equations consume our mind. We are convinced that this worldly success is the key to our happiness. And here we go, constantly pushing, striving, and hustling—trying with all our might to be enough, to find happiness, success, acceptance, and contentment. Eventually, our words are saying all the right Christian lingo, but our heart and passions are completely removed from wanting to know who Jesus Christ is.

> This people draw near me with their mouth, and with their lips do honour me, but have removed their heart far from me, and their fear toward me is taught by the precept of men. (Isaiah 29:13)

I didn't think I was doing anything wrong. I was trying to better myself, be perfect. Yet, my quest to be perfect like Christ had also transitioned into being perfect in the world as well. And they were both leaving me unnourished. My heart had become weighed down with the stress of the world, chasing success, and living my dreams—that I wasn't leaving room for Christ.

> Until Jesus Christ is the obsession of your heart, you'll always be looking to mere men to meet needs only He can fill.
>
> —Leslie Ludy[1]

Just as the quest of trying to be equal to Christ is impossible, our quest of pursuing alternative equations for happiness and satisfaction also leaves us empty handed. Fitness, beauty, money, straight A's, a decorated house, traveling the world—they are all expendable.

Are any of these things bad to have or even to want? No, absolutely not. That's why they are so enticing. Because they can be "good" things. Taking care of our bodies, having a beautiful home for our family—they are good! However, when they become the foundation on which we hinge our happiness, success, and contentment, that's when we have a huge problem.

We don't know what tomorrow brings. In an instant, everything and anything could be gone.

Ask someone who has ever experienced a traumatic event. Ask someone who has been let go from a successful job. Ask an athlete who has experienced a devastating injury. Ask someone who has lost a loved one. Nothing in this world is guaranteed.

These equations become a bottomless pit and endless circle, especially when you are a perfectionist. We live in a world where there will always be someone who is prettier, skinnier, makes more money, has a cleaner house, has flatter abs or who has more social media followers. It's endless.

So instead of finding true and lasting happiness, we become slaves, imprisoned and chained.

———

THE PERFECT LIE SEPARATES US FROM CHRIST. IT CONVINCES US THAT WE NEED TO BE LIVING PERFECTLY ENOUGH THAT WE DON'T ACTUALLY NEED CHRIST'S ATONEMENT.

Still to this day, I don't know how this happened. Maybe this didn't happen to you, but for me, I developed a skewed reality of what Christ's Atonement actually was.

In my ignorant and innocent teenage mind, I had created fear around the need to use Christ's Atonement. Since Christ was perfect, He became the only qualified person that could perform the Atonement. In my mind, the reason He was worthy enough to perform the Atonement was because He didn't need it. And, well, if I needed to be perfect and equal to Christ, then I needed to do all I could to "not need" the Atonement either.

Do you see what happened right here? I separated Christ and the Atonement as if they were two separate things. But they aren't. The *Atonement* shouldn't even stand alone as one word. Christ is the one with the power. Christ atoned for our sins. The *Atonement* was something Christ did, but the *Atonement* isn't what holds the power—Christ is.

Russell M. Nelson describes this in his talk "Drawing the Power of Jesus Christ into Our Lives."

> It is doctrinally incomplete to speak of the Lord's atoning sacrifice by shortcut phrases, such as "the Atonement" or "the enabling power of the Atonement" or "applying the Atonement" or "being strengthened by the Atonement." These expressions present a real risk of misdirecting faith by treating the *event* as if *it* had living existence and capabilities independent of our Heavenly Father and His Son, Jesus Christ.[2]

This is where things got really messy and jumbled.

In my mind, I measured how well I was doing in this life according to how often I "needed" to use the "Atonement," or how often I needed to repent.

My heart hurt every time I thought about the magnitude of Christ's suffering, and I feared how much Christ had to suffer for my sin and weaknesses. Because of this, I tried hard to be perfect, so I didn't have to use His Atonement. Somehow, this made me feel better about myself and what Christ had to go through.

Can you see how twisted and destructive this kind of reality is? This isn't truth! Trying hard to "not need Christ's Atonement" doesn't do us any good. In fact, it completely ruins the entire purpose of why Christ went through what He did in the first place. Christ has already suffered, bled, and died for each of us. His Atonement doesn't hold power, but He does! And He is ready at all time, and in all seasons to help us. Yet my attempt at "trying not to need the Atonement" was merely keeping me away from accessing Christ's divine power and intervention every day of my life.

This is the kind of thinking that keeps people from repenting. This kind of thinking breeds shame when we make mistakes. This kind of thinking makes people leave the Church, because confessing is too hard. This kind of thinking completely separates us from our Savior, who has already saved us. Trying not to need Christ or His Atonement is like a giant WIN for Satan.

Did Christ tell us to "be ye therefore perfect, even as your Father which is in heaven is perfect" (Matthew 5:48)? Yes, He did. But nowhere did He ever say that we needed to do it without Him. Nowhere did He say that we needed to be equal to Him. Nowhere did He say, "Try hard not to need my help. And then when I die, I'll make up the rest."

That's not how Christ works!

My quest for perfection wasn't about what Christ could make me. It was about what I thought I needed to be in order to get to heaven. It was about trying to be enough. It was a constant measurement of "How fast did your child learn the ABCs?" "What size are your jeans?" and "How many family vacations have you taken this year?" For years, I was glorifying being busy while worshipping checklists. There was no room for error, no room for flaw, not enough time, not enough talent, and never any grace!

- The Perfect Lie made me a slave to a life that wasn't fulfilling, happy, or joyful.
- The Perfect Lie made me believe that I was failing every day.
- The Perfect Lie made me believe that being skinny would make me happy.
- The Perfect Lie made me believe that there wasn't any room for error, failure, or flaw.
- The Perfect Lie had me breeding shame into every sin and mistake that I made.
- The Perfect Lie made me exhausted, worn down, and hopeless.

- The Perfect Lie made me believe that I needed to try hard not to need Christ or His Atonement.
- The Perfect Lie made me believe that I needed to be "just like Christ."
- The Perfect Lie had me living a life without Christ's grace.

Unlike the Perfect Lie, Christ's truth is simple. To his disciples, He declared: "Follow me, and I will make you fishers of men." To each of us, Christ declares: "Come, follow me and I will make you. I will make you all that you need to be. I will make you more.

"I will make you enough."

CHRIST'S TRUTH

Me + Christ = More

NOTES

1. Leslie Ludy, *Answering the Guy Questions: The Set-Apart Girl's Guide to Relating to the Opposite Sex* (Eugene, OR: Harvest House, 2009), 8.
2. Russell M. Nelson, "Drawing the Power of Jesus Christ into Our Lives," *Ensign*, May 2017, 40.

EIGHT

Me + Christ

The word *perfect* is used in the Bible one hundred and twenty-three times between the Old and New Testaments.

Knowing that the Bible was written thousands of years ago, let's take a look at the first way Satan has morphed and distorted God's truth. When those of the Old Testament spoke of perfection, it didn't have the same meaning or connotation as today. In the Greek translation, the word *perfect* doesn't mean "flawless." The Greek meaning of *perfect* is defined as "brought to its end, finished." It was also translated as "whole" (my favorite of the definitions).

In Frank F. Judd Jr.'s religious study "'Be Ye Therefore Perfect': The Elusive Quest for Perfection," he states:

> The Hebrew word translated as "perfect" is *tamim* and means, among other things, "whole, sound, healthful" and "having integrity." The Septuagint—the Greek translation of the Old Testament—uses the word *teleios* . . . to mean perfect in the sense of "complete" and "entire."[1]

Neither the Greek or Hebrew translation to *perfect* actually means "without flaw, fault, or imperfection."

Surely then, our quest to become "perfect" isn't about becoming "flawless" or "faultless." Instead, it is a quest to become "whole" with Christ. To become "sound, finished, and brought to our end" with and by Christ.

The Perfect Lie had me believing that it was up to me to change by myself, and that I, by sure grit, needed to be perfect. I thought if I could work harder, do a little more, be more disciplined, then do more again—that somehow I would eventually get there. If I could just *try* harder, I would *be* better.

But you tell me one place in the scriptures where Christ says, "Oh. Sorry! You just aren't working hard enough. You definitely messed up way too much. There's no hope. Your efforts are inadequate, and you'll probably never be enough." He never taught that everything in your life needs to be perfect, without flaw, failure, or mess-ups.

Can you imagine your Savior, the man who bled and died for you, saying that? No way. Christ's love is unconditional, in every way and in every season. In fact, Christ's life was surrounded with those who were broken, hurt, diseased, and weak. Yet here I was, derailing every attempt He made to heal me because all I could see was how I was falling short of earthly expectations.

My entire life I believed I only had two choices.

1. To forever keep carrying the chains of perfection, until maybe one day I will have finally worked hard enough and became flawless and equal to Christ.
2. Free myself from the expectation of perfection, abandon my faith, and leave the gospel.

Yet the entire time, there was another option, an option of truth and freedom.

3. **Let Christ change me, and live a life growing by the power of His grace.**

As the clatter and clamor of life bustle about us, we hear shouting to "come here" and to "go there." In the midst of the noise and seductive voices that compete for our time and interest, a solitary figure stands on the shores of the Sea of Galilee, calling quietly to us, "Follow me."

—Joseph B. Wirthlin[2]

Christ has never expected us to be perfect on our own. His plan is a plan of joy, happiness, and hope. My fears of never being enough, my guilt for failing, my despair that I'd never measure up—those feelings aren't from Christ, nor are they from living the gospel of Jesus Christ.

Those feelings are from Satan. And if we are feeling them, then we are listening to a lie.

Christ's truth is simple. "Come unto me and let me change you."

For my grace is sufficient for thee: for my strength is made perfect in weakness. (2 Corinthians 12:9)

The Perfect Lie tells us that we must reach perfection on our own, without Christ. Which is why perfectionism is so destructive and suffocating. It demands immediate perfection. Right now. Today. It twists the truth "be ye therefore perfect, even as your Father which is in heaven is perfect" and convinces us that we need to live a life being equal to Christ, to be perfect like Christ—rather than *perfect with* Christ.

Christ's truth and quiet plea to each of us is: "Come unto me" for "my grace is sufficient." My grace is sufficient to make you anything you could ever want to be. My grace is sufficient to change you.

No matter how weak, broken, or flawed you may be, Christ's grace can transform you. With Christ, nothing is impossible—no heartache, no sin, no trial.

This is Christ's truth, "add my perfection and power to your life and I will make you anything you want to be. I will heal you. Change you. I will make you more. And I will make you enough."

Me + Christ = More
Me + Christ = Enough

Perfection is possible, but only if we develop an intimate relationship with Christ. Godly perfection is possible. It is a hopeful quest. But Godly perfection requires a union of ourselves with Christ, joined together as one. It requires that Christ's perfection and power lives inside of us. Godly perfection isn't living without flaw, it is living flawlessly with Christ.

WE OBTAIN GODLY PERFECTION WHEN WE ALLOW CHRIST TO LIVE INSIDE OF US. THE MORE INTIMATE WE ARE WITH CHRIST, THE MORE WE BECOME WHOLE IN CHRIST, "AT ONE" WITH CHRIST, AND PERFECT IN CHRIST.

The more Christ fulfills the cravings of our souls, the more he changes our taste capacities from the inside out. The more we walk with him, the more we want him. The more we taste of him, the more we enjoy him. And this transforms how we live and what we live for.

—David Platt[3]

Let's look at another scripture that expounds upon the misunderstood scripture: "Be ye therefore perfect, even as your Father which is in heaven is perfect" (Matthew 5:48).

In the book of Mormon, Moroni writes of a similar admonishment. Yet his words give us deeper insight and perspective of how this "perfecting" process works. Moroni writes:

> Yea, come unto Christ, and be perfected in him, and deny yourselves of all ungodliness; and if ye shall deny yourselves of all ungodliness, and love God with all your might, mind and strength, then is his grace sufficient for you, that by his grace ye may be perfect in Christ; and if by the grace of God ye are perfect in Christ, ye can in nowise deny the power of God.
>
> And again, if ye by the grace of God are perfect in Christ, and deny not his power, then are ye sanctified in Christ by the grace of God, through the shedding of the blood of Christ, which is in the covenant of the Father unto the remission of your sins, that ye become holy, without spot. (Moroni 10:32–33)

This scripture immediately gives us a different insight. Let's start that first sentence again, but replace *perfected* with *whole*.

"Yea, come unto Christ, and be *whole* in Him."

Notice it doesn't say *like* Him. It says *in* Him. While studying this concept more thoroughly, I discovered that it's a key concept in learning how to fully use Christ's Atonement. Let's look at a few other scriptures where Christ invites us to literally let Him live and be *in* us.

> Abide in me, and I in you. As a branch cannot bear fruit of itself, except it abide in the vine; no more can ye, except ye abide in me. (John 15:4)

> That they all may be one; as thou, Father, art in me, and I in thee, that they also may be one in us. . . .
>
> And the glory which thou gavest me I have given them; that they may be one, even as we are one:
>
> I in them, and thou in me, that they may be made perfect in one. (John 17: 21–23)

The next few scriptures give us a symbolic reference from Christ Himself who taught that His Spirit is the very substance we need to partake of.

> I am the living bread which came down from heaven: if any man eat of this bread, he shall live for ever. (John 6:51)

> I am the bread of life: he that cometh to me shall never hunger; and he that believeth on me shall never thirst. (John 6:35)

> Whosever drinketh of the water that I shall give him shall never thirst; but the water that I shall give him shall be in him a well of water springing up into everlasting life. (John 4:14)

> Except ye eat the flesh of the Son of man, and drink his blood, ye have no life in you.
> Whoso eateth my flesh, and drinketh my blood, hath eternal life; and I will raise him up at the last day.
> For my flesh is meat indeed, and my blood is drink indeed.
> He that eateth my flesh, and drinketh my blood, dwelleth in me, and I in him.
> As the living Father hath sent me, and I live by the Father: so he that eateth me, even he shall live by me. (John 6:53–57)

Interesting, isn't it? The concept of partaking of Christ, joining with Him so that He literally lives inside of us. He is the water, the bread, and the tree. Not only do we need to seek Christ, but we need to let His words nourish our souls. We need a yearning desire to partake of His power, to feast upon His words, and to drink His Spirit as though it truly is the living waters! If we do not abide *in* Him and be whole *in* Christ, we will not and cannot be perfected in Him.

But as we *seek* Christ and *partake* of Christ, we will naturally *become* like Christ. Line upon line, we become perfected! For this is the natural consequence of accessing His grace.

Let's go back to Moroni's words.

> *By his grace ye may be perfect in Christ*; and if by the grace of God ye are perfect in Christ, ye can in nowise deny the power of God. (Moroni 10:32; emphasis added)

Grace is the only way we can become "perfected." Notice the last sentence. "If by the grace of God ye are perfect in Christ, ye can in nowise deny the power of God." When I read that, I realized that not only is grace the only way we can become perfected, but as we become perfected we will not be able to deny God's or Christ's power. We will know that His grace changed us, because we will miraculously become more than we ever could by hard work or discipline alone.

WHAT IS GRACE?

In a BYU devotional titled, "In the Strength of the Lord," David A. Bednar states:

> I suspect that you and I are much more familiar with the nature of the redeeming power of the Atonement than we are with the enabling power of the Atonement. . . . Most of us clearly understand that the Atonement is for sinners. I am not so sure, however, that we know and understand that the Atonement is also for saints—for good men and women who are obedient and worthy and conscientious and who are striving to become better and serve more faithfully. I frankly do not think many of us "get it" concerning this enabling and strengthening aspect of the Atonement, and I wonder if we mistakenly believe we must make the journey from good to better and become a saint all by ourselves through sheer grit, willpower, and discipline, and with our obviously limited capacities.[4]

I don't know why, but I always equated grace with mercy, as if it was forgiveness for falling short. I thought grace was almost a pardon given by Christ when we get to the judgment seat. My first awakening and real "aha" moment to this newfound choice that I could have in life came when I listened to and studied Brad Wilcox's speech "My Grace Is Sufficient for Thee."

Brad unveiled and eloquently portrayed Christ's grace in a way I had never even heard before.

> Growth and development take time. Learning takes time. When we understand grace, we understand that God is long-suffering, that change is a process, and that repentance is a pattern in our lives. When we understand grace, we understand that the blessings of Christ's Atonement are continuous and His strength is perfect in our weakness. When we understand grace, we can, as it says in the Doctrine and Covenants, "continue in patience until [we] are perfected."[5]

Christ's grace is not something that is earned at the end of mortality; it is an actual enabling, changing power that we can access every single day. When my life fell apart, I had no idea how Christ could heal me. I had always understood how to repent for my sins, and I knew that Christ's Atonement was supposed to cover heartache, pain, disappointment, and weakness, but I never knew how this worked. The Bible Dictionary defines *grace* as the "*divine means of help or strength*, given through the bounteous mercy and love of Jesus Christ" (emphasis added). Grace is not mercy, but because He is merciful and loves us unconditionally, He is willing to come to even to the depths of hell to be with us, unite with us, and bring us back home. Because of His mercy and His power, perfection is available to all!

When Christ pleads with us to know Him and prophets admonish us to read about Him, it's with full purpose to gain and access Christ's power. It's not to check something off our Christian checklist. God's commandments have the full purpose of gaining the blessing of Christ's power. When we walk with, talk to, and learn of Christ, we allow Christ into our lives to change us.

As Wilcox goes on to say:

> Grace is not a booster engine that kicks in once our fuel supply is exhausted. Rather, it is our constant energy source. It is not the light at the end of the tunnel but the light that moves us through the tunnel. Grace is not achieved somewhere down the road. It is received right here and right now. It is not a finishing touch; it is the Finisher's touch.[6]

CHRIST'S REDEEMING POWER ALLOWS US TO BE FORGIVEN OF OUR SINS, BUT CHRIST'S GRACE CHANGES OUR DESIRES, APPETITES, AND HEART SO WE NO LONGER HAVE THE DESIRE TO SIN.

I recently had a conversation with a man who had a heavy pornography addiction. He told me how, in the depths of his addiction, he believed he could never change. Without the help of his bishop, he tried for years to overcome this heavy addiction on his own. He didn't want to be involved with it; he knew it was destroying his life, and he knew he was sinning. He felt awful, horrible, and worthless. Yet no matter how hard he tried to stop, he couldn't beat his natural appetites and fell into temptation every time it presented itself.

Eventually, the addiction became so heavy that he finally surrendered and knew he needed help. Going to the bishop's office was one of the hardest things he had ever done. The shame and worthlessness that he felt was unbearable. However, when he finally took the courage to reach out for true repentance, everything changed. It took time, but as he faithfully went through true repentance for his sins and became devoted to knowing Christ, his appetites started to change. As each month passed, he grew stronger and stronger. Today, the temptation isn't even appealing to him. His heart has changed. His natural appetites have changed. Sure, he still has to be cautious and remember that he isn't invincible to sin—but an appetite for sin that seemed too impossible to overcome has now been replaced with the strength of the Lord.

Do you remember Paul? Paul, originally called Saul, was an active participant in persecuting Christians. The sins Paul committed were serious. Yet this one time persecutor become one of the greatest missionaries that has ever walked the face of the earth. There are few that can compare to the testimony, faith, and resilience that Paul had. His mark in the New Testament has surely changed my life, as I know it has for thousands and millions of others. How is that possible? How is possible for someone whose heart is so hard and darkened to become full of light, passion, and goodness?

The answer is Christ's grace.

> When we become followers of Jesus, we make a decided break with our old way of living and take a decisive turn to a new way of life. As Christ begins to live in us, everything begins to change about us. Our minds change. For the first time, we realize who God is, what Jesus has done, and how much we need him. Our desires change. The things of this earth that we once loved we now hate, and the things of God that we once hated we now love.

—David Platt[7]

When Christ fill our hearts, our very nature changes. The more we come to know Christ, the more intimate He becomes in our souls, the more His perfection lives inside of us. We suddenly want to be kinder to others. We judge others less often, because we see them as Christ does. We feel accepted because we feel Christ's acceptance for us. With Christ, we naturally develop Christlike attributes, and our desire to be obedient to Christ's commandments become easier.

Me + Christ = Greatest Desire to Be Obedient
Me + Christ = Extend More Forgiveness

Me + Christ = A Greater Self-Esteem
Me + Christ = Patience to Endure Trials
Me + Christ = Faith and Courage to Try Something New
Me + Christ = Strength to Withstand Temptation
Me + Christ = Desire to Share the Gospel

When Christ stands beside us and lives within us, our eyes becomes His eyes; our hands, His hands; and our heart, His heart.

Christ's grace multiplies, transforms, and expands our efforts, weaknesses, and shortcomings.

As I studied Jesus's life, I realized this was the continuous theme in His entire ministry: taking the weakest things of this earth and using His power to transform them into something miraculous. Christ never asked us to give more than we have to give. In fact, God's entire purpose is to give us shortcomings, weaknesses, and inadequacies because He wants us to know Christ and so He has given us reasons to come to Him.

> The Lord God showeth us our weakness that we may know that it is by his grace, and his great condescensions unto the children of men, that we have power to do these things. (Jacob 4:7)

When five thousand people needed to be fed and the only food available was a meager five loaves of bread and two fishes, the Lord didn't say it wasn't enough. He didn't look away or condemn the offering. No! He took that imperfect and inadequate amount of food and, thanking God in prayer, poured His power and grace upon it, magnifying that weak offering into a miraculous feast. Not only did He make it enough to feed thousands, but there was more food than those five thousand people could eat.

When those at the wedding feast ran out of wine before the night was over, Christ didn't judge. He didn't laugh and stand there wondering who the heck had planned the party. No, He knew there was a problem, and even if it was something as simple as running out of wine, He cared. And He made a miracle happen. He told the servants to fill the stone jugs with what they did have, which was only water, and then to trust Him. And He turned the water into wine. But not just any wine. He transformed that water into the very best wine they had had all night.

When Christ's grace flows into our lives, everything seems to go better. Our time is more efficient. We have more energy to accomplish our goals and plans. We are more creative. Our weakness becomes enough.

Our shortcomings are adequate. We actually have time to rest and rejuvenate. Everything changes when we live by and through Christ's grace.

Me + Christ = Weakness Strengthened
Me + Christ = Talents Magnified
Me + Christ = Better Time Management
Me + Christ = More Efficient
Me + Christ = Priorities Fall into Place
Me + Christ = Bigger Dreams
Me + Christ = Successful

Christ's grace is the power that enabled Moses to part the Red Sea and lead the Israelites out of bondage. It enabled David to kill Goliath with just one rock. Christ's grace is what enabled Nephi, a man proclaimed as a poor writer, to bring forth the greatest writings and chapters of the Book of Mormon that would lead God's greatest generation in the latter days. Christ's grace is what enabled a weak, uneducated fourteen-year-old boy to be bring forth the restored gospel of Jesus Christ. If Christ's grace is sufficient for them, it is sufficient for you as well. No matter your mess, your sin, your weakness, or your shortcomings—Christ's grace can make you more. He can make you perfect.

The Savior has "all power" in heaven and on earth. He has power to cleanse, forgive, and redeem us; power to heal us of weakness, illness, and heartache; power to conquer Satan and overcome the flesh; power to work miracles; power to inspire and strengthen us; power to deliver us from circumstances we can't escape ourselves; and power over death. When the Apostle Paul said, "I can do all things through Christ which strengtheneth me," he was describing grace.

> Grace is divine power that enables us to handle things we can't figure out, can't do, can't overcome, or can't manage on our own. We have access to this power because Jesus Christ, who was already a God, condescended to endure the bitterness of a fallen world and experience *all* physical and spiritual pain.
>
> —Sheri Dew[8]

Christ has never asked us to give more than we have to give. Instead, He asks, pleads, and invites us to learn of Him, come to Him, trust Him, and let Him make us more. He pleads for us to put Him first, to partake of Him and know Him, to walk where He is walking, and He will make us equal to anything and everything He calls us to do. For with Christ we are more. We are powerful. We are enough!

Me + Christ = Contentment
Me + Christ = Peace
Me + Christ = Acceptance
Me + Christ = Gratitude
Me + Christ = Faith
Me + Christ = Loved
Me + Christ = Happy

When Christ quenches our souls and fills our hearts, we have everything we need. With Him, we are accepted, loved, happy, and successful. With Him, we will always have a friend. When we have Christ next to us, even the most lowly of circumstances becomes enough. With Christ, we can have gratitude in all seasons of life, and live satisfied, contented, and happy no matter what comes our way.

NOTES

1. Frank F. Judd Jr., "'Be Ye Therefore Perfect': The Elusive Quest for Perfection," in *The Sermon on the Mount in Latter-day Scripture*, ed. Gaye Strathearn, Thomas A. Wayment, and Daniel L. Belnap (Provo, UT: Religious Studies Center, Brigham Young University; Salt Lake City: Deseret Book, 2010), 123–39.
2. Joseph B. Wirthlin, "Follow Me," *Ensign*, May 2002.
3. David Platt, *What Did Jesus Really Mean When He Said Follow Me?* (Carol Stream, IL: Tyndale House Publishers, 2013), 33.
4. David A. Bednar, "In the Strength of the Lord" (Brigham Young University devotional, October 23, 2001), 2–3, speeches.byu.edu.
5. Brad Wilcox, "My Grace Is Sufficient for Thee" (Brigham Young University devotional, July 12, 2011), 5, speeches.byu.edu.
6. Ibid.
7. David Platt, *What Did Jesus Really Mean When He Said Follow Me?* (Carol Stream, IL: Tyndale House Publishers, 2013), 35.
8. Sheri L. Dew, "Sweet Above All That Is Sweet," *BYU Magazine*, Fall 2014, 26; italics in original.

NINE

We Were Born Broken

There is no doubt that understanding Christ's grace was the first big breakthrough I needed in order to free myself from the Perfect Lie. And since I first shared this idea to find true freedom, I knew that I needed more truth. I needed more understanding as to *why* I needed Christ's grace. I knew I needed it because I was weak. I obviously wasn't obtaining perfection on my own. But I didn't fully understand how I could access this power every day of my life. I had no idea that once I did, it would forever change the way I live.

President Ezra Taft Benson stated:

> Just as a man does not really desire food until he is hungry, so he does not desire the salvation of Christ until he knows why he needs Christ. No one adequately and properly knows why he needs Christ until he understands and accepts the doctrine of the Fall and its effect upon all mankind.[1]

I thought I knew a decent amount about the Fall of Adam, but as I read those words by a modern-day prophet, I could feel God pushing me to dig deeper.

I knew there was more to understanding this false perception of perfection. I understood now that I had been living a life without Christ's grace. Yet I still couldn't understand or find solace in the fact I felt so weak. Weakness still felt like failure. I knew that grace could absolve my sins. But what could it do for my human weaknesses? I knew I needed more answers, more truth, and the Fall seemed to be the place God was leading me.

UNDERSTANDING SPIRITUAL DEATH AND THE FALL OF ADAM

For a minute, let's reflect on the truth that you and I are children of God. We are spiritual beings who not only lived with our Father before we came to this earth, but we walked, talked, and interacted with Him—a Father who had endless power, who loved us and taught us. While in the pre-earth life we knew our worth. We were confident in God and Christ. We trusted Them, and because we trusted Them, we knew that receiving a physical body was the only way we would become like Them. Yet to do this, we would have to enter mortality. And in order to enter mortality, each of us would have to experience spiritual death. We'd have to be cut off from God and His influences and forget everything.

Growing up, I had always equated spiritual death exclusively with our own personal sin. Is this true? Partly, yes. When we willfully disobey God, we separate ourselves from Him and His influences. However, what I hadn't realized or understood was the fact that we each experience spiritual death by two different avenues. That's right, there's not just one way that we spiritually die, but two. The first came to us due to the Fall and the second we experience by our own disobedience.

Since I was in Primary, I learned, sang, and memorized the second article of faith. I knew that "men will be punished for their own sins, and not for Adam's transgression."

This repetitive teaching, although correct and true, made me disregard the impact that the Fall actually had on each of us. In my mind, "Adam fell that men might be, and men are that they might have joy" (2 Nephi 2:25). I knew that the Fall allowed us to come to earth, but I also knew that Adam would be judged for his choices and I will be judged for my choices. In my uneducated mind, there wasn't a lot more to it. Maybe you were much more advanced as a teenager, but I never truly understood how the Fall affected me.

Bruce R. McConkie summarized the Fall this way:

> Adam broke the law of God, became mortal, and was thus subject to sin and disease and all the ills of mortality. We know the effects of his fall passed upon all his posterity; all inherited a fallen state, a state of

mortality a state in which temporal and spiritual death prevail. In this state all men sin. All are lost.[2]

Did you catch that? The effect of Adam's Fall affects all of his posterity. I guess in a sense I knew this, or at least bits of it. But what I didn't know is that the moment each of us were born into this world we inherited all of the following consequences due to the Fall:

1. We experienced spiritual death and eventually a temporal death. (Alma 42:9)
2. We became fallen and lost forever. (Alma 42:6)
3. We were cut off from the presence of the Lord. (Alma 42:7)
4. We became carnal, sensual, and devilish by nature. (Alma 42:10)
5. We were placed in a state of opposition. (D&C 29:39)
6. We were placed in a position to be tested by difficulties of life and temptations of the adversary. (Moses 6:48–49)
7. We received conflict within us. (See 2 Peter 1:4 and Ether 3:2.)
8. We became unworthy before God. (Ether 3:2)
9. We were born into the natural man. (Mosiah 3:19)

In Wendy Ulrich's article, "It Isn't a Sin to Be Weak," she expands on the reality of entering mortality and the consequences of the Fall by stating:

> As mortals we are born helpless and dependent, with various physical flaws and predispositions. We are raised and surrounded by other weak mortals, and their teachings, examples, and treatment of us are faulty and sometimes damaging. In our weak, mortal state we suffer physical and emotional illness, hunger, and fatigue. We experience human emotions like anger, grief, and fear, We lack wisdom, skill, stamina, and strength. And we are subject to temptations of many kinds.[3]

I remember the first time I wrote all of these consequences out on paper I was mind-blown. *Um, OK! So before I have even had an opportunity to sin, I'm already carnal, unworthy, sensual, prideful, and placed in an state of opposition?* Yep. And here I was stressed because my child had three popsicles for breakfast! Not that I'm promoting sugar for breakfast—I'm all about children successfully eating raw organic vegetables. I'm just saying that maybe, just maybe, perfectionism had me beating myself up and feeling like a failure over things that didn't really matter. I mean maybe I could ease up a bit because my son happened to watch *Toy Story* on repeat for one entire day.

When God began teaching me this doctrine in new light, in a new way, I realized that before I even had a chance to be perfect, I was already extremely broken.

Even if I could have somehow been equal to Christ, completely perfect, never sinning—that still wouldn't have been enough to get me into heaven. Even if I had been able to pull off the impossible and walked this earth sinless, I still would be separated from God due to the consequences of the Fall.

The harder I worked to try and understand the Fall, the more I couldn't believe what I had been doing. All those times I beat myself up for not performing perfectly, all those times I felt like a complete failure because I needed help or fell short, every time I couldn't keep my brokenness together and someone saw—it's as if I believed I was born perfect, and I was trying with all my might to stay that way. But the truth is, I never came here perfect in the first place.

Oh, the lies Satan tells us. Let's just all agree to cast him out forever, because none of us have time for him.

So, we each experience spiritual death by two sources, our own personal sin and our natural man (those consequences we inherited from the Fall). But spoiler alert: Christ's Atonement can redeem us from both of these consequences. However, how we overcome them is different. Let's first look at how we overcome being separated from God by our own personal sins.

OVERCOMING PERSONAL TRANSGRESSION (SIN)

All have sinned, and come short of the glory of God. (Romans 3:23)

Overcoming that kind of sin was a gospel principle that I was highly versed in: Repentance.

The Primary answer for overcoming sin is repentance. It is the key by which we can become clean again. This process goes as follows:

OVERCOMING SIN

1. Repent
2. Feel Sorrow for Sin
3. Confess
4. Abandon Sin
5. Make Restitution
6. Commit to Righteous Living

These steps are pretty straightforward, and repenting is a principle that most Latter-day Saints are familiar with. When we exercise repentance, we are able to access the redeeming power of Christ's Atonement. He then forgives us of our sin, and we become clean. This process is something we will continually have to do every day and every week, as "no unclean thing can enter into his kingdom" (3 Nephi 27:19).

Part of this process also includes being baptized by immersion and covenanting with God. Renewing those baptismal covenants weekly through the sacrament enables us to continually become clean and pure. We must personally appeal to Christ and take His name upon us every week to repent of our personal sins. This process of continually becoming clean by repentance is powerful and needed in order to access so much of who Christ is and to overcome spiritual death—but what about the natural man and the consequences that befell us because of the Fall? Being baptized, repenting, and partaking of the sacrament cleanses us from our own transgressions and sin—it's all part of the changing process, but that alone does not entirely cleanse us from the inherent consequences of the Fall.

When Nicodemus approached Jesus Christ, Jesus told him that "Except a man be born of water *and of the Spirit*, he cannot enter into the kingdom of God. . . . Ye must be born again" (John 3:5, 7; emphasis added). This concept obviously confused Nicodemus as he thought Jesus Christ was being literal, but we learn that physical baptism isn't enough to gain our salvation.

There are two separate issues that we are dealing with here: (1) sin, and (2) the natural man or our weakness. We often think that sin and weakness are the same, but they aren't. They are two different elements that we as mortals are trying to overcome.

> We commonly think of sin and weakness as merely different-sized black marks on the fabric of our souls, different severities of transgression. But the scriptures imply that sin and weakness are inherently different, require different remedies, and have the potential to produce different results.
>
> —Wendy Ulrich[4]

Now that we took a refresh on how Christ helps us overcome our personal sin, let's dive into overcoming the consequences of the Fall, the natural man, and our weaknesses.

OVERCOMING THE CONSEQUENCES OF THE FALL (NATURAL MAN/WEAKNESS)

If repentance is the antidote for sin, then what is the antidote for mortal weakness? The redeeming power of Christ is what we access when we repent, then the enabling power, or Christ's grace, is what we have to use and access in order to overcome our weakness and the natural consequences of the Fall.

> And the Lord said unto me: Marvel not that all mankind, yea, men and women, all nations, kindreds, tongues and people, must be born again; yea, born of God, changed from their carnal and fallen state, to a state of righteousness, being redeemed of God, becoming his sons and daughters;
>
> And thus they become new creatures; and unless they do this, they can in nowise inherit the kingdom of God. (Mosiah 27:25–26)

Where repentance changes us and cleanses us from our sin, the following steps are the antidote for overcoming the consequences that befell us because of the fall. Or in other words "our weaknesses."

OVERCOMING WEAKNESS

1. Be born again
2. Born of God
3. Changed from our carnal and fallen state to a state of righteousness
4. Redeemed of God
5. Become new creatures
6. Show humility
7. Exercise faith in Christ
8. Accept our state of human weakness
9. Keep trying
10. Trust God
11. Ask God to help us change
12. Obey
13. Be patient
14. Come unto Christ

Again, Christ's grace isn't some mercy that we obtain at the end of this mortal life; it's the literal power and antidote that we have to access in order to triumph over spiritual death. It is not enough to show up to the judgment seat clean of sin—we have to show up there changed. We have to become "new creatures" and "born again." We have to have received "the image of God engraven upon [our] countenances" (Alma 5:19). Accessing Christ's grace is the only way we can truly do this.

When you live life by the Perfect Lie, you have two goals: (1) to never commit sin, and (2) to simultaneously live your Christian checklist perfectly. However, even if you were to do this, it's not enough, because God's plan requires change. We didn't come to earth to see how far we can make it on the world's ladder of success—but instead our purpose is growth. It's to see how close and intimate we can become with Christ. It's not just learning how to avoid sin but transforming into someone who no longer has a desire to sin.

Overcoming our second state of spiritual death requires a rebirth, a second baptism that doesn't cleanse us physically from sin but that cleanses and purges us of the consequences of the Fall. When we experience this mighty change, "We are made alive in Christ. . . . We talk of Christ, we rejoice in Christ, we preach of Christ" (2 Nephi 25:25–26).

This kind of change is not something we can do alone. It requires complete and total dependency on Jesus Christ. It requires a desire to change. And it requires a steadfast desire to continue to be purged and changed. It takes persistence, patience, and diligence in actively coming unto Christ.

In David A. Bednar's talk "Ye Must Be Born Again," he elaborates beautifully on spiritual rebirth when he states:

> We are instructed to "come unto Christ, and be perfected in him, and deny [ourselves] of all ungodliness" (Moroni 10:32), to become "new creature[s]" in Christ (see 2 Corinthians 5:17), to put off "the natural man" (Mosiah 3:19), and to experience "a mighty change in us, or in our hearts, that we have no more disposition to do evil, but to do good continually" (Mosiah 5:2). Please note that the conversion described in these verses is mighty, not minor—a spiritual rebirth and fundamental change of what we feel and desire, what we think and do, and what we are. Indeed, the essence of the gospel of Jesus Christ entails a fundamental and permanent change in our very nature made possible through our reliance upon "the merits, and mercy, and grace of the Holy Messiah" (2 Nephi 2:8). As we choose to follow the Master, we choose to be changed—to be spiritually reborn.[5]

D. Todd Christofferson said: "Being born again, unlike our physical birth, is more a process than an event. And in engaging in that process is the central purpose of mortality."[6]

When we fail to access Christ's grace, when we fail to accept our weakness with humility and love, we cannot experience the change we need to experience during mortality. Thus, accepting our weakness is a vital part of our salvation. As Henry B. Eyring stated: "Those who do not see their weaknesses do not progress."[7] Thus, the more we try and keep all our pieces together, the less we allow ourselves to be changed by Christ's grace.

To be changed by grace and to receive this essential kind of rebirth that is needed, we have to let Christ in to every part of our mess. We have to lay our natural man at His feet. Spiritual rebirth is not something we can just work tirelessly alone at. Changing ourselves into who God knows we can become can't be done by sheer grit or by hustling after a checklist. This kind of change can only be brought about by a power that far exceeds mortality. This kind of change can only happen by that divine infinite power and grace that resides with our Savior, Jesus Christ.

But as Brad Wilcox testifies, this is the miracle. "The miracle of grace is not just that God can take us out of slavery, but that He can take the slavery out of us."[8] But He can't if we keep running from our brokenness, and He can't if we don't let Him in.

I get it. No one likes to feel like a mess. No one likes to feel like they're broken or "less than." But guess what? Whether or not we like it, we are broken. We were all broken the moment we got here. Don't let Satan breed shame into your mess. Because the truth is, each one of us is fighting the Fall. Each one of us is fighting sin and transgression. Each one of us is fighting weakness. I'm a mess, you're a mess, and even that perfect person at church you think has no problems—yep! They're a mess too! And we are all desperately in need of Christ's grace.

Wow! Can you imagine what this mind shift did for an overachieving, keep-it-all-together, "conceal don't feel" kind of girl? This reality and humble reminder that we really are all so broken helped me find hope and joy. It helped me not feel so bad about my mess, about my brokenness. And it should help you feel better about yours too!

This extended knowledge of the Fall helped me realize that despite my belief that everyone else seemed to be keeping it altogether, they probably weren't. The human experience demands that we feel weak, broken, and mortal. The human experience demands that we feel all of the emotions, even if we logically know the answers. The human experience demands that we know pain, heartache, suffering, joy, love, and patience. And each one of us is experiencing it. Yes, we each experience it in different ways, but no one is escaping it.

For some reason, this knowledge shattered my determination to prove I was enough and even my fear of not being enough. Because the truth is, I'm not. I'm not enough. (At least without Christ I'm not.) Accepting my brokenness gave me the freedom to stop pretending and start living. I stopped shamefully hiding and laid it all at Christ feet—the bad days, the lazy days, the days I didn't read my scriptures, the days I get short-tempered or impatient, the days I cry and yell at God. I could finally accept all of it. And not just accept it, but breathe in it. Because all of it doesn't determine my worth. My worth is infinite. Our brokenness isn't a reflection of our true selves, but rather it's a reflection of our natural man. It's a reflection of those afflictions and consequences that we were sent here to overcome with Christ's help. Beating ourselves ruthlessly over our flaws doesn't do us any good, for *we* are not the enemy, the natural man is—and it always has been.

> For the natural man is an enemy to God, and has been from the fall of Adam, and will be, forever and ever, unless he yields to the enticings of the Holy Spirit, and putteth off the natural man and becometh a saint through the atonement of Christ the Lord, and becometh as a child, submissive, meek, humble, patient, full of love, willing to submit to all things which the Lord teeth fit to inflict upon him, even as a child doth submit to his father. (Mosiah 3:19)

SHEDDING THE NATURAL MAN

Robert L. Millet stated: "So what characterizes the natural man? Simply stated, the natural man is the man who remains in his fallen condition; he has not experienced a rebirth."[9]

I'm a visual person, and once I realized that I needed to stop fighting against myself, and instead fight against my natural man, I started imagining my natural man as a thick layer of mortar that's built around each of us. Inside each of us is the gold, diamond, or silver waiting to come forth, but if our outside layers don't experience heat, pressure, refinement, even some cracking and chipping, then how can the natural man ever fall off of us?

Have you seen a large tree whose bark is shedding? In order to grow, the original skin of the tree has to break, crack, and fall off. Although painful and uncomfortable, this must happen, even to us, if we are going to grow. We must allow our natural man to shed in order for us to be changed. We must allow our tribulations, trials, weaknesses, and inadequacies to aid in the spiritual expansion needed to break through our debilitating layers of the natural man: pride, self-doubt, fear, false truth, anxiety, and ignorance.

Let's be honest. Being stretched, humbled, and tried is never fun; it's uncomfortable to change—however, letting go of these prideful layers and accepting our mortal brokenness is the only way we can become the magnificent wonder God created us to be!

This life is a test. We were sent here so that we could become like that powerful God and Father that we left. We knew that when we accepted God's plan of progression, and we knew that coming to this earth would be a time for us to prove to God our worthiness and our desire to live with Him again.

> Prove yourselves unto me that ye are faithful in all things whatsoever I command you, that I may bless you and crown you with honor, immortality, and eternal life. (D&C 124:55)

> And we will prove them herewith, to see if they will do all things whatsoever the Lord their God shall command them. (Abraham 3:25)

Not only did God have a purpose to prove and test us, but we learn in multiple Old Testament scriptures that as mortal beings, we are here to learn, to grow, and to be refined. Each of us will be asked to walk through our own furnace if we are to become the changed being that God knows we can become.

> And I will bring the third part through the fire, and will refine them as silver is refined, and will try them as gold is tried. (Zecharaiah 13:9)

> When he hath tried me, I shall come forth as gold. (Job 23:10)

These beautiful scriptures teach us that, like gold, our refinement process requires heat and pressure. Just as coal is transformed into diamonds, this kind of change requires the substance to break down and change its original properties and turn into something new. It is the purity that comes from extreme heat and refinement that makes gold even more precious. It is the diamond that comes from coal that has great price. And so it is with us, the person that we become as a result of our trials is of greater concern to God. Now, I don't mean to say that He doesn't care about who you are right now, because He absolutely does. But His priority while you are on this earth is to help you change into the person He knows you can become. And God knows that putting you in situations that lead you to His Son, the one person who can change you, is the only way to do this!

While studying the Fall, I became intrigued by the concept of being "broken." I starting noticing how broken each and every person in the scriptures felt at one time or another. Studying this topic made me wonder why I had tried so hard for so long to hold all of my broken pieces together. With awakened spiritual eyes, I started seeing my trials in new light. Too often, I looked at my trials as failures rather than refinement. When Wes lost his job, I questioned where he had fallen short. I looked for where he had failed. When I chose to close my business, I felt like a complete failure. I saw where I was weak, how I had overpromised and underdelivered. I beat myself up for not being healthy enough to handle the stress that came with operating my own business.

With new eyes (and maybe some maturity), I could see that the changing of careers for both Wes and me didn't have to be failures at all. They were trials and learning experiences and chances for refinement. These "failures" ended up being our greatest blessings. Our trials aren't always connected to who we are or what we have done. Some trials simply come because this is mortality, and we were born into a state that was going to experience situations that would help us learn, grow, and change.

Not only did God have a purpose to prove and test us, but we learn in the Old Testament that as oral beings, we are here to learn, to grow, and to be refined. But the truth is, living by perfection doesn't allow for growth or for deviations. My "perfect life" was a one-way path that I wanted to control. I was so set on my projected destination that I didn't stop to consider that the place God had in mind might actually be better. I didn't see that the deviations from my plans were actually divine course corrections. I couldn't see how learning experiences and trials could place me in situations that allow me to be refined and purified. The Perfect Lie had me fighting against any resistance or deviation that came my way. But how can we grow when we fight so hard against God? How can we grow when we fight against trials, pain, or tribulations? How can we ever become the gold we're meant to be when we continually fight against the fire and heat? We can't. We simply can't.

I've learned now that surrendering to God's will and those things I can't control are pivotal to my growth. They are pivotal to our faith and to the person God needs us to become. God isn't there so we can command Him to serve us and to serve our needs and wants; God is there so we can learn to completely, totally, and happily serve Him.

Having this change of heart isn't easy, but it's a whole lot easier once you realize how broken you are, and how dependent you are on God and Christ in the first place.

NOTES

1. Ezra Taft Benson, "The Book of Mormon and the Doctrine and Covenants," *Ensign*, May 1987.
2. Bruce R. McConkie, *The Promised Messiah* (Salt Lake City: Deseret Book, 1978), 244.
3. Wendy Ulrich, "It Isn't a Sin to Be Weak," *Ensign*, April 2015, 32.
4. Ibid, 30.
5. David A. Bednar, "Ye Must Be Born Again," *Ensign*, May 2007, 20.
6. D. Todd Christofferson, "Born Again," *Ensign*, May 2008, 78.
7. Henry B. Eyring, "'My Peace I Leave with You,'" *Ensign*, May 2017, 16.
8. Brad Wilcox, *Changed through His Grace* (Salt Lake City: Deseret Book, 2017).
9. Robert L. Millet, "Putting Off the Natural Man: 'An Enemy to God,'" *Ensign*, June 1992.

TEN

Pride: The Sin behind Perfectionism

I was hurting and my heart was in pain. Yet as I stepped outside my door, I could feel that mask pulling itself onto my face. The forced smile and the "I'm good" nod. *Don't let others see. Be strong. Don't ask for help. Keep smiling. Keep it together and say the right thing.*

Do you know this mask? I hope not. But if you made it this far in my book, chances are you've been affected, someway, somehow by the Perfect Lie. This mask, to always be strong—it's the last leg that holds the Perfect Lie together. So far we've discovered the following truths:

1. Our quest should never be about striving to be equal to Christ, but rather to have an intimate relationship with Him.
2. Calling upon Christ's grace is the only way we can overcome spiritual death and become "new creatures."
3. We were never perfect to begin with, and (due to the Fall) each one of us need to overcome brokenness.

Once I discovered these truths, I knew that the last big step to overcoming the Perfect Lie was to identify the sin behind it. Because each of Satan's lures is rooted in a type of sin in one way or another—even perfectionism.

Since mankind has walked this earth, there has been an ever growing sense of pride to be strong, to always be OK. That culture norm of survival of the fittest has created a false truth that we must be strong and always put together. I have never been good at asking for help. Consciously and maybe subconsciously I equated the need for help as a sign of failure. I didn't want to be seen as "not strong enough." 'Cause gosh dang it, I was strong! I needed to be strong. I wanted to prove I was strong. And I feared being weak. I feared looking "less than." But did I think that was being prideful? No way! I thought it was part of the plan!

If you were to ask me ten years ago if I thought I was a prideful person, I would have told you no. I had a real gift for self-deprecation, and I didn't believe that anything I did was that great. I didn't think I was pretty, talented, or wise. I was involved with a lot of extracurricular activities, but my perfectionist mind showed me clearly where I lacked and where I could do better. Because of that, I was rarely confident in what I was doing. So surely, I wasn't prideful? I didn't boast about anything I ever did, because nothing I ever did was good enough. My drive to be strong didn't seem prideful, it seemed necessary to survive this world and to be enough. Christ could handle even the worst of trials and tribulations. Surely I needed to handle mine as well.

President Ezra Taft Benson said this about pride:

> Pride is a very misunderstood sin, and many are sinning in ignorance. . . . Most of us think of pride as self-centeredness, conceit, boastfulness, arrogance, or haughtiness. All of these are elements of the sin, but the heart, or core, is still missing. The central feature of pride is enmity— enmity towards God and enmity toward our fellowmen.[1]

The direct definition of *enmity* is "hatreds toward or hostility"—and in the past as a "good girl," I would have never believed that I had any hatred toward my fellowmen, let alone God. That seems hard to connect with. However, as I have dug deeper into this journey, enmity is much more than hatred. It's anything that is in opposition against something else. It's a barricade, a wall.

Perfectionism is pride of the highest order, with a variety of consequences. Perfectionism fears men more than God, it separates us from connection, and it distances us from Christ's grace.

PERFECTIONISM FEARS MEN MORE THAN GOD

The proud depend upon the world to tell them whether they have value or not. Their self-esteem is determined by where they are judged to be on the ladders of worldly success. . . . Pride is ugly. It says, "If you succeed, I am a failure." If we love God, do His will, and fear His judgment more than men's, we will have self-esteem.

—Ezra Taft Benson[2]

I never wanted to care what others thought of me. However, even the tiniest slight against my character or integrity drove my fears out of control. That same feeling I felt as a third-grader of not wanting to be "less than" carried itself through so many parts of my life.

My need to always say yes to favors? It was because I feared hurting someone's feelings; I feared that they would be mad at me. I feared that they would think I was rude or inconsiderate. When clients would push me on work deadlines or try to negotiate unreasonable prices, I let it slide and worked on their terms because I feared that they wouldn't be happy with me, that they would stop using me, or that they would tell others that they weren't satisfied with my work. I didn't want my business to fail, and I didn't want my clients to get upset with me. I feared "what men thought."

The fear of "what men thought" motivated everything I did. Checking emails, working out, doing laundry, cleaning the house, and spending quality time with my son all started taking precedence in the morning. Little things that I felt I had to do slowly pushed my scripture study later and later into the day. For a long time, I would try to read the scriptures after I crawled into bed. But my body, spirit, and mind were exhausted, and it was hard to really get anything out of my study. Like I said before, my clients, family, friends, and worldly to-dos were getting the very best part of my day, and God was getting the worst. Once I started working through the night, scripture study wouldn't happen at all. I overbooked myself because I was afraid what the consequences would be if I said no to the things of the world. I feared that I wouldn't make enough to support my family, that I would fall behind everyone else, that I wouldn't be a perfect mom, and I feared what others thought of me. So I feared just about everything more than God. And, eventually, the consequences became impossible to ignore. I was overbooked, stressed, and sleep deprived, and my spirituality and my physical body were dwindling away from lack of nourishment.

Like President Benson said, this pride is often ignorant. It was for me. It wasn't until my health was gone, exercise was gone, my business was gone, and having more children wasn't happening that I realized how much I drew from these things for my worth. This kind of pride inhibits us from being who God meant for us to be. When our value and worth doesn't come solely from God, we can't do His work. We can't be all that God intended us to be. God wants us to be bold. He needs us to step into our power. He needs voices, and truth. And unless we stop fearing where we land in the world of success or stop fearing that we will be seen as less, we can never do His work. In short, our worth must come first and foremost from the knowledge that we are children of God.

When my life became still, I had no choice but to find my worth in solely being a daughter of God. And when I did, everything changed. All of sudden, it mattered a lot less what others said about me because now I know whose I am. I know that nothing I do, or don't do can take that away from me. I don't fear what men say about me. OK, maybe I do a little. I'm still human. Even writing this book has been a little scary. But at the end of the day, I'm learning to care most about what God has called me to do.

I was sharing my story a few weeks ago, when a few people approached me afterward, each saying similar things:

"Wow. You just shared some very hard, personal, ugly things. That's a very vulnerable place to put yourself in."

"That takes a lot of courage to share what you did. I don't think I could."

"How are you just OK sharing all of this? Don't you worry about what others will think?"

Here's the thing. I don't worry like I use to. This is the amazing thing about Christ and Heavenly Father. They are changing me. When I came to this place of knowing who I was, God started asking me to do hard things. He has probably asked you to do hard things too. But now, I understand that my experiences aren't attached to my worth, and I don't see them as failures or flaws. Sharing and opening myself up this way doesn't scare me like it used to, because now I know who I am. My experiences and shortcomings aren't who I am. I am God's, and I know where I stand with God. That's all that matters.

Sharing some of this years ago would have killed me. I would have been terrified. Now? Ask me anything you want, I'll tell you. Isn't that freedom? My relationship with God, doing what He has asked me to do matters more than anything else in this world. It matters more than a house, making money, or being seen as "cool."

The pride of fearing what others think or where you fall on the world's ladder of success barricades you from God. It keeps you from your power, and it separates you from who God needs you to be.

PERFECTIONISM SEPARATES US FROM EACH OTHER

During the six months that Wes and I lived apart (he was starting his job in California while I waited for our house to sell in Arizona), I decided to take Jaks and move to Utah to be with family and so that it was closer for Wes to visit us every other weekend. The day our house sold, I packed Jaks back into our car and drove from Utah to Arizona to pack our belongings. Due to unforeseen circumstances, no one else could come with me until the following weekend, but by that point I needed to have the entire house packed up and ready so it could be loaded into U-Hauls.

Although I was extremely grateful that my husband and I would finally be back together, this move became one of the hardest periods of my life. It was midnight when I pulled into our home in Arizona. Jaks was asleep, and I walked into our cute home we had worked so hard to build. It wasn't our dream house, but it was home, and it had been good to us. As I walked in, everything was quiet and clean—obviously, since it was being shown and we weren't living there.

I walked upstairs to our master bedroom, where I laid Jaks on the bed and crashed. My entire body hurt due to the chronic health issues I was facing, and my chest could barely expand because of my anxiety. Everything felt so overwhelming.

I don't understand why I felt the need to try to be strong or why I didn't ask for help. But the only person I even told that I had sold our house was my best friend.

The next morning, I bought as many boxes as I could. With Jaks in tow, I went home and tried to decide where to start. I'd walk from one room, to the next, to the next. I'd start putting things in boxes, but then I'd become too overwhelmed to finish. My heart was breaking and my anxiety was paralyzing. Around 10:30, the phone rang and it was my best friend.

"Tiff, have you started packing yet? I'm coming to help! What do you need?"

I swallowed back the tears and tried smiling.

In my "everything is fine" voice I tried cheerfully saying, "Oh, are you sure? Do you have anything else today? That's so nice. I'm doing OK, but I definitely would love to see you! You don't need to help, but please come over so I can see you and at least say goodbye."

Liar. I was a big, fat liar. Why was asking for help so hard? If there is anything I have learned from this experience, it's that God loves us and blesses us even when we don't deserve it.

The next thing I knew, my dear friend had called ten more people to come help. Each showed up ready to pack and clean my house. As each one of them left, I could hardly talk, I was so overwhelmed with gratitude. After everyone left, I put Jaks to bed only to hear a knock at the door.

I opened it up to find the sister missionaries.

"Hi, Sister Webster."

It completely took me off guard. I had only had one interaction with the missionaries and I didn't know why they were there.

"Hi, Sisters. How can I help you?"

"We are actually here to help you! We have one hour before we need to be back to our apartment, and God told us to come here. How can we serve you?"

Tears started streaming down my face. These sisters had no idea I was moving. They didn't know that earlier that morning I was wallowing in complete anxiety, paralyzed by everything that needed to be done. I invited them in and they finished sweeping and mopping my floors. When they left, I fell to my knees and poured my heart out to God. I could feel His love and His arms around me. He knew me. And in that moment I felt my Savior's love in a powerful and impactful way.

WE CAN'T DO THIS ALONE

Today, Satan is breeding shame and judgment into our lives at a rapid rate. We're scared and fearful, and we wonder if we will ever measure up. We spiral when we make mistakes and are convinced that there isn't any hope. We hurt; we ache.

In the past, neighbors knew each other's heartaches, pains, and trials. Today, Satan is doing all he can to keep us busily living alone. We come and go out of our homes, never seeing our neighbors, rushing from one task to another. We put on smiles, briefly waving, trying to be strong, all while scrolling through the surface of each other's lives.

Yet how many of us really know the depths of each other's mortal journey? How many of us know that our neighbors sit, just as we do, in the corners of their rooms in tears, fighting the darkness of this world alone?

God is love. And God is connection. There is a reason His second greatest commandment is to love your neighbor. He knows that we need each other. He knows that we need connection. Perfectionism is a champion at shutting people out. Satan doesn't want us to experience love or connection, so he convinces us to pridefully wear the mask of "I'm fine, I'm strong, and everything's OK." He tells us to keep smiling. Keep hiding. Keep all the pieces together. He tells us that asking for help is weakness, and that nothing weak makes it in this world.

However, keeping our pain and brokenness hidden from the world is not strength. It's pride—pride in its highest form that separates us from God in the most isolating ways.

This doesn't mean we should spew every bad thing that ever happens to us—doing that only increases our negativity and helplessness. Sometimes I wonder how to keep the balance of being open and vulnerable versus just being a depressing crazy lady who talks about every negative thing in her life. And don't misread what I'm saying. We do need courage, and we need strength. But never asking for help, always being OK, or not knowing how to receive service separates us from connection and from love.

When Jesus was alive and people wanted to serve him, it would have been so easy for Him to look at them and say, "Um, I'm the Savior of the World. I'm perfect in every aspect of the word. Maybe you should go serve someone else who needs it more. Because I'm fine."

That almost sounds absurd, right? Can you imagine the Savior turning down someone's service? Even as much as the Savior served, loved, and gave, He also taught how to graciously, meekly, and humbly receive.

Yes. Jesus lived, died, and rose again for all of us. He cleansed the leper, healed the man at the pool of Bethsaida, gave life to the daughter of Jairus, and wept with Mary and Martha when hearing of their brother's death. However, Christ also humbly received even the humblest acts of service. He asked John the Baptist to baptize Him, even when He had no need to be baptized. When Mary came to wash Christ's feet with her tears, He didn't turn her service away or get awkward or uncomfortable. The disciples were even angry and felt it a waste to use such expensive spikenard. Yet the Lord rebuked them and He graciously let Mary express her gratitude and love as He accepted her service in the most meek and humble way He could.

When your child offers to help you with something that you really don't need help with, do you turn them down? Or do you see it as your child expressing their love for you? That they really see you? I think it is a sign that a person is looking outside of their own needs and seeing the needs of another that should be cultivated. The Lord doesn't need our service for Himself. He gives us the opportunity to be His hands, not only to bless others' lives but our life as well.

Christ always allowed others to love Him and to serve Him. And by doing so He gained an even greater love for them. Being the one who receives allows us to feel Christ's love and understand more fully just how much He does love us. Meekness and humility are two of the greatest Christlike attributes we can emulate.

If we never take off the mask of perfection, we miss this opportunity. If we are always "fine," we don't allow ourselves to fully feel the love of our Savior. Instead, we become isolated, disconnected, and alone.

That first night I pulled into our house alone with Jaks, I remember fervently pleading and praying that God would make me stronger, that He would take my anxiety away and make me capable. If He did, maybe I wouldn't need help.

Obviously, my prayers weren't answered the way I had begged them to be. Instead, He sent angels. He sent miracles. He brought loving arms to embrace me, working hands that made my load light, thoughtful messages that gave me hope, extra prayers from those I love, and tender mercies that helped me recognize His love for me. He sent witnesses that He indeed knew me. All immeasurable blessings that far exceeded what I would have gained had He simply given me strength to do it alone.

Accepting help often feels like weakness. It's hard and humbling to let others clean our house, help us with a resume after we lose our job, scrub our dirty bathroom, or see us in a moment of exhaustion and tears. It's hard letting others see us in our less than ideal circumstances. However, it's these situations that allow God's love to grow more than it ever could if we were continually strong. It's the brokenness that unites us. It's the tragedy, trials, and imperfection that connect us.

Think of a moment when you have felt the most loved. I can guarantee they were moments of brokenness, moments of failure, weakness, sickness, or struggle; incidents where pride wasn't barricading connection. Brokenness requires us to help pick up each other's pieces. It requires us to love, be loved, and unite in love. It requires service and less judgment. Yes, it takes courage to stand in your mess, but when we each let our walls down and stand in our mess together, judgment quickly fades away, and love is able to unite us.

As disciples of Jesus Christ we have been commanded to become one in mind, heart, and spirit. We have been commanded to build Zion, united together in one purpose. This kind of unity takes connection and how can any of us become one mind, one heart, and one spirit when we aren't willing to share our heart, mind, and spirit with each other? It's simply not possible.

> I beseech you, brethren, by the name of our Lord Jesus Christ, that ye all speak the same thing, and that there be no divisions among you; but that ye be perfectly joined together in the same mind and in the same judgment. (1 Corinthians 1:10)

> Stand fast in one spirit, with one mind striving together for the faith of the gospel. (Philippians 1:27)

> And the Lord called his people Zion, because they were of one heart and one mind, and dwelt in righteousness. (Moses 7:18)

This is why Satan loves when we're silent about our trials. He loves shaming us into solitude. God, on the other hand, knows that we need each other. He knows that we need each other's brokenness if we are ever to become united in Christ! For God's greatest work can only be done through love and connection.

I am grateful for a God who answers prayers, not how we want, but rather how we need. I've learned in a personal and sacred way how blessed we are to receive. By receiving, we find meekness. And meekness allows us to find Christ!

PERFECTIONISM DISTANCES US
FROM CHRIST'S GRACE

I was so afraid of how I would be received if I was broken, that I rarely admitted how messed up I really was. The shame of being unworthy and flawed made me hide from God. I hated that I made the same mistakes over and over. I hated that I couldn't seem to get my family to have daily scripture study. I felt so much guilt and shame about messing up that I didn't often lay my brokenness at Christ's feet. I couldn't stand to go to Him with the same weaknesses and trials that I hadn't been strong enough to conquer on my own. I only cried out for help when I had failed.

But Christ isn't there to help us only when we have failed. He doesn't want to be there only after we have tried on our own. He wants to be there every step of the way. Perfectionism shamefully looks at needing help as failure, and it ignorantly tries to do life alone. Or at least this is how perfectionism affected me. I thought I was going to Christ. I thought I was laying it down at His feet, but the truth is, I never fully did. In the morning, I'd often wake up thinking about everything that needed to be done, rather than thinking about how excited I was for Christ to help me. Evening prayers pleading for strength were a much more frequent occurrence than beginning my day asking for help before I even began.

Accessing Christ's grace continually requires a mind, heart, and soul that knows its dependency on Christ. It requires a heart that loves Him more than men. It requires a soul that earnestly aches for more of Him. By keeping our brokenness hidden, we don't allow Christ to touch it. But when we let go of pride, when we accept our nothingness and total dependency on Him, then He can step in and repair our broken pieces. Christ's greatest work comes from the weakest things of the earth.

> At the same time came the disciples unto Jesus, saying, Who is the greatest in the kingdom of heaven?
>
> And Jesus called a little child unto him, and set him in the midst of them,
>
> And said, Verily I say unto you, Except ye be converted, and become as a little children, yet shall not enter into the kingdom of heaven.
>
> Whosoever therefore shall humble himself as this little child, the same is greatest in the kingdom of heaven. (Matthew 18:1–4)

I have always loved this story and lesson that Christ taught us: to become as little children again. If you can think of the most humble, meek, and submissive child you can, this is ultimately what Christ needs us to be. He needs us to wake up already needing Him. Humility isn't an easy thing, but when we see humility and meekness as strength, when we let go of our pride, we actually become stronger than we could ever imagine. Admitting that we need help, every single day, allows our lives to become powerful. It allows us to live day by day in Christ's grace.

NOTES

1. Ezra Taft Benson, "Beware of Pride," *Ensign*, May 1989.
2. Ibid.

PART THREE

Living by Grace

ELEVEN

Jesus First

OK, so now what? This is the question I remember asking God. Now what, God? Now that I understand the truth, now that I've unraveled the lie of perfection, now that I know how badly I need Christ's grace—how do I change? How do I live a life that is rooted in the power of Christ's grace?

These same questions that I myself asked God are the very same questions that I get asked weekly. I've received hundreds of emails and messages with stories of those who have fallen into the same trap, the same vice, and they too want a different way, a different life. And they ask me where to start and what to do.

I don't have all the answers. I don't have all the tools. Growing by grace is an intimate experience between God, Jesus Christ, and each of us individually. And I'll be the first to admit that I don't have this completely figured out. However, in the next few chapters, I will share what tools and experiences I have learned as I have chosen to start living by grace. And the first step to all of it, is choosing Jesus Christ.

We must decide if Christ is who we want to serve. Do you want Him to be your master? This doesn't mean you aren't going to mess up, or that you aren't going to sin. This doesn't mean that you aren't going to have days where you binge on Netflix instead of reading your scriptures. No, you'll have plenty of days like that. But are you all in for trying? Is Jesus the one who you want to serve, the one you want to know, and the one you will keep trying, facing, growing, and learning for?

> If you have not chosen the kingdom of God first, it will in the end make no difference what you have chosen instead.
>
> —William Law[1]

I decided He was for me. I've seen the alternate choices. I've seen where life takes you when you don't have Christ. For every one of us, someday, we will all hit rock bottom. Someday Satan will come with his all mighty hail, and his mighty storm will beat upon us. And what will we do if that comes and we haven't chosen Jesus? What are we going to do when the earth shatters and the fear and darkness get thicker? What will we do, if like the five foolish virgins, we have no oil in the last days?

> A successful life, the good life, the righteous Christian life requires something more than a contribution, though every contribution is valuable. Ultimately it requires commitment—whole souled, deeply held, eternally cherished commitment.
>
> —Howard W. Hunter[2]

It may not be easy. Scratch that, it won't be easy. Things may not make sense. But decide today that Jesus Christ is who you want and that He matters more than anything else. Decide that today is the day your life changes forever. It did for me.

Living by Christ's grace means putting Jesus first. This doesn't mean doing it perfectly, every time, but trying hard to have our hearts put Him first. Once we have done that—there is no looking back. I have found the best way to fully put Him first is to pattern the teachings He taught the disciples. Choosing to be a disciple of Jesus Christ is not an easy quest. But it's worth it. There are three things that we can do to help us be disciples of Christ and enhance our ability to live by His grace: we must leave our nets straightway, never take our eyes of Him, and love Him with all of our heart, mind, and strength.

STRAIGHTWAY LEAVE OUR NETS

And Jesus, walking by the sea of Galilee, saw two brethren, Simon called Peter, and Andrew his brother, casting a net into the sea: for they were fishers.

> And he saith unto them, Follow me, and I will make you fishers of men.
>
> And they straightway left their nets, and followed him. (Matthew 4:18–20)

What an unwavering commitment. They "straightway left their nets." They didn't say, "Let us finish what we are doing." The Savior called them, and they left their worldly concerns immediately to follow Him. Do we do this? I know I didn't. When my life was consumed with keeping up with the world, I in no way "straightway left" my net. The trickiest part about this was that Satan used good things to keep me distracted from putting Christ first. My thoughts were consumed with taking care of my family, living our dreams, growing relationships, and friendships—all good things, but centering my life on Christ should always have been the priority.

I find it interesting and no coincidence that the New Testament gives us a few more examples of this same kind of scenario, yet with different results.

Now let's take a look at this same invitation that Christ gives three other men—yet each with a different response.

> And it came to pass, that as they went in the way, a certain man said unto him, *Lord I will follow thee whithersoever thou goest.*
>
> And Jesus said unto him, Foxes have holes, and birds of the air have nests; but the Son of man hath not where to lay his head.
>
> And he said unto another, Follow me. But he said, *Lord, suffer me first to go and bury my father.*
>
> Jesus said unto him, Let the dead bury their dead: but go thou and preach the kingdom of God.
>
> And another also said, *Lord, I will follow thee; but let me first go bid them farewell, which are at home at my house.*
>
> And Jesus said unto him, No man, having put his hand to the plough, and looking back, is fit for the kingdom of God. (Luke 9:57–62; emphasis added)

Seems a little harsh, doesn't it? For the first man, Christ emphasizes that He Himself doesn't even have a home or a bed to lay His head. To the second man, who wanted to bury his father who had died, Christ makes it pretty obvious that not even burying his father was more important than preaching the kingdom of God. And the same to the last. That not even family is more important than Christ.

Why? Why would Christ give us such extreme examples about the price of true discipleship? Well, from my experience, it's because those very things, those righteous, even eternal things were the very things that got in my way of fully following Him. My dreams for my family, for myself, and for how I wanted my life to look got in the way of my devotion to the Lord.

Wes and I are both the oldest of our families. When we got married, Wes had six other siblings living at home and I had three. Our families are extremely involved—athletically, musically, and everything else under the sun. When we got married, we were both working and going to school full time. Then after work, we'd find ourselves trying to space out time between families, and trying our hardest to support each of our now nine siblings. We loved them all, but trying to find balance into separating the time equally was challenging, and we weren't perfect at it. But we tried hard to do what we could. Most days, we didn't get home until 9:30 or 10 p.m., and we were up early the next day doing school, work, and family all over again.

Before becoming parents, Wes and I found ourselves reading every parenting book we could get our hands on. Books about sleep training, sign language, baby products, breastfeeding, organic food, discipline. I was working full time, Wes was finishing school, and what little time we had became consumed with making sure we were doing all we could to offer the best and most perfect circumstances we could for our son. We loved him, and we wanted him to thrive.

Now, are school, work, and family all important? Is giving our son a healthy optimal living environment important? Yes. Absolutely. But were we having family scripture study? Not really. Were we reading our scriptures individually? Barely. Making time for it seemed like an endless battle. I knew that we needed to be having family scripture study, and I felt guilt every day that we didn't. Yet it wasn't a nonnegotiable priority in our schedule, and the world's demands made it too easy to slip through our day.

Everything that we were doing, all that was occupying our time—they were good things. Yet, slowly, Christ became the middle of our priority list, when school, work, and even family became higher priority than spending consistent time with Christ each day.

Peter and Andrew's example of "straightway leaving their nets" shows what devoted disciples they really were. In the end, isn't this what any righteous Christian wants? To be devoted this way?

When I had a real "come to Jesus" talk with the Lord, I realized that I had too many nets. There were too many other things that were keeping me from fully straightway following the Savior.

Nets come in all shapes in sizes. Some of them are addictive and destructive, like pornography, alcohol, drugs, or immorality. But nets can be anything—debt, work, meetings, checklists, birthday parties, holiday preparation, sport teams, social media—anything that keeps us from putting Christ first. Do you know the scores to the latest basketball game more than you know the scriptures? Do you know every crease, flaw, and wrinkle on your body more than you know Christ? Do you prepare for your kids' birthday parties more than you prepare for the Sabbath day?

It may sound harsh, but it's true. Those things that we are passionate about aren't bad, but they become nets when the priority of Christ no longer takes precedence in our day.

Straightway leaving our nets is a life time journey that we will work on every day. Am I perfect at this? No. But I am much better than I ever was before. I see now when nets are keeping me from being spiritually fed. I see where I need to cut back and when I'm running faster than I should. I've also had a miracle happen: when Jesus is the obsession of my heart, I still have time for all the things I originally did anyway.

I'm not even kidding! Sure, I'm making sacrifices, but God is a merciful God, and when we put Him first, He helps us make time for the things we are passionate about. He helps us chase our dreams, strengthen our relationships, be better parents, and even have time to ourselves to watch a basketball game or movie. It's exciting when you let God govern your time!

KEEP OUR EYES ON JESUS

I love Peter. He is without a doubt my very favorite disciple of all time. Who else would have the courage to try and walk on the water? Sometimes I think he gets a bad rap, but if you read carefully, could anyone have greater faith than him?

What courage and faith he had to ask Christ if he too could try and walk on the water. For those first few steps, He looked at Christ. He saw the Lord and had confidence in Him. He saw the power in Christ, which gave Him the courage to also step out onto the water, a feat that no man in the history of this world has ever been able to achieve besides Christ Himself.

With full faith, Peter stepped onto that water, "to go to Jesus" (Matthew 14:29).

What happens next, I believe, is the most crucial part of the story:

But when he saw the wind boisterous, *he was afraid.* (Matthew 14:30; emphasis added)

In order for Peter to see the wind and the waves, his eyes had to leave the Savior's. Peter was walking miraculously on the water; however, once his eyes were removed from Christ, it is then that doubt and fear overcame him. He didn't doubt while he was looking at Christ. He had faith. It is only when he saw what he was up against that he began to sink.

And beginning to sink, he cried, saying, Lord, save me. (Matthew 14:30)

If you feel fearful, worried, or stressed, take a minute to evaluate what your eyes are fixed on. Are they fixed on the giant dark waves of death, finances, sickness, other's trials, or the world news? If so, look back to the Savior. Take your eyes off of the tempest and train your eyes on the man that causes "even the winds and the sea [to] obey Him" (Matthew 8:27).

I know for me, Facebook is a huge trigger. I know it can be used for good, but it's one of those dark waves that send me sinking every time. When I get sucked into my news feed, I see too many harsh words, GoFundMe pages for the most heart-wrenching tragedies, death, war, children starving, sexual abuse. I can't be ignorant to these horrible tragedies; I understand they need our attention. However, the days I get myself sucked into Facebook too long are the days I end up in my closet crying, completely overcome by fear.

When Wes gets home, he knows exactly what has happened and always asks me, "Why did you look? Why did you get sucked into the fear?" It is then that I usually have to dive back into my scriptures and refocus on Christ and His goodness, His peace, and His hope.

How often does this happen to us, though? The world is loud, noisy, and distracting. There is a constant demand to go here and be there. It's no wonder that men's hearts are failing them. Nothing in this world seems possible, and it all seems overwhelmingly fearful. Without our eyes fixated on Christ, there is no way we can navigate through these last days in hope and faith! When we, like Peter, step out onto the tempest-tossed waters and see the Lord sustaining us, we are confident. We cannot take our eyes off of Him for a moment; we cannot afford to.

LOVE THE LORD WITH ALL YOUR HEART

After Christ died, the disciples were at a loss for what to do. Naturally, as most of us would, they found themselves back fishing. The disciples were looking to Peter for what to do, and I'm sure that Peter, in complete agony and with a grieving heart, innocently went back to the one place that had always provided him comfort. He went fishing. And the disciples followed him. They fished all night, and by morning they had still not had any success.

> When the morning was now come, Jesus stood on the shore: but the disciples knew not that it was Jesus.
>
> Then Jesus saith unto them, Children, have ye any meat? They answered him, No.
>
> And he said unto them, Cast the net on the right side of the ship, and ye shall find. They cast therefore, and now they were not able to draw it for the multitude of fishes.
>
> Therefore that disciple whom Jesus loved saith unto Peter, It is the Lord. Now when Simon Peter heard that it was the Lord, he . . . did cast himself into the sea. (John 21:4–7)

In one second, when Christ influenced them, they had more fish than they could ever even pull into the boat. That's what happens when Christ is with us. When we are following Him, when we are walking and talking beside Him, He makes what we are doing successful.

The next scene of the Savior's interactions with sweet Peter is one that pierces my soul. Every time.

> When they had dined, Jesus saith to Simon Peter, Simon, son of Jonas, loves thou me more than these? He saith unto him, Yea, Lord: though knows that I love thee. He said unto him, Feed my lambs.
>
> He said to him again the second time, Simon, son of Jonas, loves thou me? He said unto him, Yea, Lord: thou knowest that I love thee. He saith unto him, Feed my sheep.

He saith unto him the third time, Simon, son of Jonas, loves thou me? Peter was grieved because he said unto him the third time, Lovest thou me? And he said unto him, Lord, thou knowest all things; thou knowest that I love thee. Jesus saith unto him, Feed my sheep. (John 21:15–17)

I ask you, as Christ has asked me, "Do you love me?"

Do you love Him with all of your being? Do you love him more than popularity, more than social media followers, sporting events, business, money, success, or traveling? Do you love Him more than someone being mad at you? Do you love Him?

Jesus isn't an afterthought only when we need help, but He should be our first thought. Our first friend. Our first listening ear. The first person we go to for advice. He shouldn't be the last resort, but the reservoir of strength that we draw from before we even begin.

> To love God with all your heart, soul, mind, and strength is all-consuming and all-encompassing. It is no lukewarm endeavor. It is a total commitment of our being—physically, mentally, emotionally, and spiritually—to a love of the Lord.
>
> The breadth, depth, and height of this love of God extend into every facet of one's life. Our desires, be they spiritual or temporal, should be rooted in a love of the Lord.
>
> —Ezra Taft Benson[3]

This kind of devotion isn't easy. If it were easy, everyone would be doing the little things. Yet it's those little things that will save our lives. When the Israelites were being attacked by "fiery serpents," they were told that they would live if only they would look upon a pole that Moses made at the direction of God, and yet there were many who refused and so died anyway because "they did not believe that it would heal them" (Alma 33:20; see also Numbers chapter 21).

To us, reading now in hindsight, it seems almost incomprehensible.

"I just don't get it. All they had to do was look? If they would have looked, they would have lived."

I don't doubt there were details about this situation that we know nothing about. However, when I think about this story, I can't help wonder what others on the other side of the veil are saying about today's generation.

"All they had to do was read their scriptures, say their prayers, and go to church. If they would have just looked to Christ, they would live. Find peace. Find joy. Why are they not looking to Him? Why can't they find time to read their scriptures?"

Lately there have been a multitude of people that have left the Church. They say that the Church asks too much, that they can't do or be all that the Church asks of them. I have felt this way before too. It's real. I get it. It can often feel like too much.

For perspective though, let's break some of it down.

There are 10,090 minutes in one week.

As a foundation, I mapped out, for me personally, what I would need to do in a week to feel like I had been successful with my devotion to the gospel.

10,080 MINUTES IN A WEEK

180 minutes for church
 90 minutes for an extra church meeting
140 minutes of daily personal scripture reading (20 min. per day)
105 minutes of family/spouse scripture reading (15 min. per day)
105 minutes of prayer (15 min. per day)
 60 minutes for Family Home Evening
120 minutes of weekly service (temple work, visiting teaching, etc.)

800 MINUTES / 10,080 = 7.4%

7.4 percent of my week! Of my time!

I know this is a rough sketch and there are items that I didn't include. I'm also not sharing this to add more guilt or make anyone feel frustrated. I simply share for perspective. When I did this activity for myself, all of a sudden I took a step back. Rather than pointing at God, telling Him He asked too much, I realized that maybe I just needed new eyes—7.4 percent of my week isn't as much as I thought it was, and heaven knows that if I was actually doing everything on that list, I would feel like I was kicking butt!

Sure, there is often more that we are asked to do, but even then it mostly likely wouldn't be much more than 10 percent of our week—10 percent of our time that God is asking us to put first, that He is pleading, begging for us to put first. And these items that He begs of us to put first, they aren't for Him. They don't give Him any gain. They are simply requests and commandments so that He can in turn bless us.

> Men and women who turn their lives over to God will discover that He can make a lot more out of their lives than they can. He will deepen their joys, expand their vision, quicken their minds, strengthen their muscles, lift their spirits, multiply their blessings, increase their opportunities, comfort their souls, raise up friends, and pour out peace. Whoever will lose his life in the service of God will find eternal life.
>
> —Ezra Taft Benson[4]

I don't know about you, but for all these blessings that He offers us—having expanded vision, a quickened mind, strengthened muscles, multiplied blessings, increased opportunities, comfort, peace, and all the hundreds of other blessings that God can pour upon us when we put Him first—it doesn't seem like He's really asking for that much in return? Does it?

Every commandment that God gives us is never for God's own gain. He asks us to keep us commandments so He can help us, so His Son can help us, and so Christ's sacrifice doesn't go in vain. God's commandments are there so that we can be changed by Christ's grace.

NOTES

1. William Law, as quoted in Neal A. Maxwell, "Response to a Call," _Ensign_, May 1974.
2. Howard W. Hunter, "Standing as Witnesses of God," _Ensign_, May 1990.
3. Ezra Taft Benson, "The Great Commandment—Love the Lord," _Ensign_, May 1988.
4. Ezra Taft Benson, "Jesus Christ—Gifts and Expectations," _Ensign_, December 1988.

TWELVE

Embracing the Broken

I t's hard to go from being an intense perfectionist to suddenly being OK with your every flaw, weakness, and failure. And this is probably the number one question that I get asked: "How did you get from perfectionism to a place of being OK with your weaknesses? How can I forgive myself for my shortcomings?"

Well, it has taken time. And it will continue to take time.

The first few months that I attempted to change my old patterns, I simply woke up each morning telling myself, "Today is a good day! But somewhere today, I'm going to fail. I'm going to fall short." For someone who hasn't struggled with perfectionism, this seems like a pretty pathetic beginning. Maybe it was, but prior to this, my mornings would start with unrealistic expectations. These expectations didn't make any room for flaws, mess ups, or hiccups. So what may seem small to some was actually a big first step for someone like me who felt like a failure every single night and who had an extreme struggle with self-forgiveness.

As I continued to start every morning with the acceptance that I was going to fail at some point during the day, I noticed that morning prayers became a lot more meaningful in my life than they ever had before. With the new expectations that I was going to fall short, I would begin my day praying specifically for Christ's grace to enable me in my weakness. I prayed for angels to be with me and for Christ's power to make me more than I was.

I also started praying for God to direct my to-do list and help me discern what His will was for me. Rather than telling Him what I needed Him to do for me, I simply asked how I could serve Him. And you know what? I found that His to-do list was a lot more manageable than mine ever had been and that sometimes it even included an afternoon moment of stillness. After a few weeks of doing this, I soon realized living intentionally by grace extended far beyond simply accepting mortality. Real power started to flow into my life when I not only accepted my weakness but embraced it wholeheartedly.

Every month as I continued to study and learn about who Christ was, the more I've come to understand the power He really has. As this has happened, I've not only been able to embrace my weakness but I've learned that there is power when we embrace every messy, hard part of our life. It has been in my brokenness, pain, and failures that I have come to know who Christ really is.

As a perfectionist, I wanted out of my weakness as fast as possible. Yes, I had read the scriptures, and yes, I knew that God was going to give us weaknesses, but I wanted those weaknesses to become strengths ASAP, and I surely didn't approach my weaknesses with love or excitement.

However, the truth is, unless we learn to love a place of weakness, we will never fully experience the complete power and strength that Jesus Christ can offer. By embracing our weakness, we step into a position that allows God to work miracles.

GOD AND CHRIST LOVE TO ENABLE THE WEAK. WHEN WE EMBRACE OUR BROKENNESS, WE BECOME DEPENDENT ON CHRIST AND OUR PROGRESS BECOMES A LIVING TESTIMONY OF HIS POWER.

Here's some news for you: Without Him, you'll never be good enough. I'll never be good enough. We are nothing without our God. He takes our little lives, laid down at His feet in the dirt, and He wrecks us with His love. When we see Him in all His beauty and let Him reshape us and fill us with His Holy Spirit, we no longer look at our failures and faults, because our eyes are drawn to see only Him.

> Unless He fills me, everything is impossible.
> *When He fills me, nothing is impossible.*
>
> —Heidi Baker[1]

When the word got out that I was writing a book, people started asking me if I had always wanted to write a book. I can't help but start laughing every time I get asked that question. Have I dreamed of writing a book? No, absolutely not. In fact, writing was always one of my greatest weaknesses. In seventh grade, my English teacher gave us an essay assignment. Getting words onto paper felt impossible to me. I did the very best I could, but it was terrible. Red pen laid visible on every single square inch of my paper, and I got an F on the assignment. My teacher told me I would never be good at English.

I believed him. I believed him for years and years. I avoided all classes that required a lot of writing. It was my kryptonite. In college, I had a real passion for my communication classes and all that they entailed. After changing my degree three times, this finally felt right. However, I was midway into the semester when I soon realized the writing demand that this degree would require of me. It felt impossible. I could see the challenge this was going to put on me and quickly started to scramble, wondering if I should yet again change my degree because I was 100 percent positive that I would fail my classes because of my weakness in writing. I sat debating back and forth what to do.

After getting back another paper with a C on it, I made up my mind. I went and made an appointment with the head of the department. He happened to be one of my teachers that semester. I sat down and told him I was changing degrees. I had tried for almost two semesters to push through the writing, but I couldn't keep going. It was only getting harder and I knew I wasn't cut out for it.

He looked at me and told me he wasn't going to let me drop out.

"Why?! You don't understand. I'm not a good writer. I never have been. I was told in seventh grade I wouldn't be good at English, and I haven't been."

How thankful I am for this wise man to this day. He walked over to me and put his arm around me.

"Tiffany, I have watched you. I hear the answers you give in class, I see the way you communicate so many great ideas. You know this stuff, and you were made to do it. Don't let the writing stop you from graduating in the degree that you love. I will stand right next to you, and I promise that before you graduate, you will learn to write. Anyone can write if they want to."

When God led me to an opportunity to write a book, I couldn't believe it! But then, of course He did. I knew, and I knew that God knew, that writing was and has been one my greatest weakness. So why *wouldn't* God make my greatest work in life be from a place of total inadequacy? I had prayed for an opportunity to be an instrument in God's hands, and I knew once I signed my book contract that this entire process would be completely, totally, 100 percent reliant upon God. And it has been. Never before have I felt so deeply inadequate. I have already spent countless hours on my knees in prayer, pleading for the next step, the next revelation, the next inspiration. Naturally, this week as I have tried to finish this chapter, I have been left with my weaknesses as I've waited for God to give me the revelation I've needed to finish. It's been stretching and hard in every way imaginable.

Yesterday, I even sat in my closet crying in desperation. I have gone to the temple, fasted, and received multiple priesthood blessings on behalf of this book. But you know what? Despite how inadequate I feel, I know, and still know even as I sit here struggling to finish, that God will not let me fail! I knew when I signed the contract that I could and would do it. Sure, I've come awfully close to questioning that confidence even this week, but I know God hasn't left me. I know His power. I know Christ's power. And I know that all things are possible with them on my side.

If Nephi could build a ship, if Moses could part the Red Sea, then surely I could write a book. Throughout this entire process, Nephi's words have echoed in my heart and mind.

> If God had commanded me to do all things I could do them. If he should command me that I should say unto this water, be thou earth, it should be earth; and if I should say it, it would be done.
>
> And now, if the Lord has such great power, and has wrought so many miracles among the children of men, how is it that he cannot instruct me, that I should build a ship? (1 Nephi: 17:50–51)

Whatever God brings us to, He will lead us through it.

God took my greatest weakness, and as promised, Christ's grace has been sufficient. That doesn't mean perfect, because I've clearly seen the way my imperfections have bled into every page, but His grace has made it enough. And because God called me to do a work that came from a total place of brokenness, that work has become a living testimony of Christ's power.

This story isn't about my weakness and failures, but it is proof that Christ's redemption, grace, and power are real! Your story of weakness doesn't have to be about you either. If you choose, it can be a miracle and testament to who Christ is.

BY EMBRACING OUR BROKENNESS, WE GIVE OTHERS THE COURAGE TO DO THE SAME.

During college, I was facing extreme anxiety. I had a kind and loving bishop who took me under his wing. I was facing some big life decisions about my collegiate athletic career, college, and dating. He started scheduling appointments for me to meet with him every Sunday, just to talk and help give me counsel.

I remember one Sunday sitting in the foyer waiting for him. Friends I knew walked past me who had also seen me there the week before. I panicked, wondering what they thought, stressing over whether they thought that I had broken the law of chastity or that I had committed some other serious sin.

I felt so much shame sitting there. I wanted to hide under the bench, and I questioned whether or not I should keep my appointments for the next few weeks.

Crazy, huh? That I was sitting there waiting to receive divine counsel from my bishop, and I was panicked about what others thought. What if I actually *had* committed a sin that I needed advice, help, and repentance for? Why should it matter?

Can you imagine if we went to church knowing we wouldn't have to experience shame? Can you imagine if, rather than holding my head down while sitting at the bishop's office, I sat there courageously, receiving high fives from anyone who passed coupled with encouraging words like, "I'm so proud of you! Whatever it is you are facing, I got your back. You got this. I'm praying for you!"? I wonder what the gospel would really be like if instead of passing each other wondering what each other's secrets are, we gave each other big hugs, embraced each other, and constantly praised each other for being at church, trying to change.

Can you imagine if we refused to judge people in church? If we went to church with intense hope and love in everything we could become, knowing that not only was I going to embrace my own brokenness, but my neighbors, family, and fellow churchgoers would also embrace me as I would embrace them? Knowing that when I went to church, I would fully have support and love, never feeling judged? There would be no shame in going to church as we are. If we saw someone waiting for the bishop, rather than awkwardly avoiding them, hoping they don't think we are judging them, we would go to them, hug them, ask them if they are OK, and let them know how much we love them, that we are proud of them, and that we are praying for them.

I don't know about you, but that's the kind of church I want to go to. And truthfully, if we were all living the gospel of Jesus Christ, this is how church would be!

EMBRACING OUR BROKENNESS ALLOWS US TO GAIN POWER. DESPITE WHAT IT FEELS LIKE, TRUE POWER COMES WHEN WE STOP RUNNING FROM OUR BROKENNESS AND INSTEAD SURRENDER TO IT.

The harder you run from fear, the greater control and power it holds over you. It's like a dark demon that chases you through the dark of the night.

But when you choose to stop, turn around and open your arms to that chasing demon, fully embracing it. That's when you gain power. Sure, it may be paralyzing and totally frightening for a minute—but all of a sudden that pain, shame, and fear will have nothing to chase, nothing to scare. And it will be powerless! Surrendering to the fear puts you in control and allows you to be free from the stress, anxiety, and worry of being chased.

I've now realized that sometimes God lets us journey into the belly of our greatest fears because He needs us to know that He is greater than any fear that Satan could ever breathe into our minds.

As I look back, I understand that the dark days of feeling worthless were actually apart of God's answers. God allowed me to walk straight into the belly of my deepest fears, not because He is heartless but because He needed me to know that He really did have me, that I was His. And no matter what I went through—He would be there, because He is my Father. I could trust Him.

When you are fighting for something eternal, you can guarantee the adversary is going to give his all. Fighting for truth, your worth, marriage, sobriety, peace, hope, and eternal life—it's not going to be easy. But guess what? You've won before. And you can do it again! Do you know why? Because the fight's already been won! Christ has already overcome. He's defeated the fear, the pain, and the heartache. The only thing left is for you to decide. Will you join Him? Will you unite with Him, every second of every day?

OUR BROKENNESS TELLS OUR STORY, AND OUR STORY IS WHAT MAKES US BEAUTIFUL.

There is a crack in everything, that's how the light gets in.

—Leonard Cohen[2]

Over a year ago, I was introduced to the Japanese art of *kintsugi*. *Kintsugi*, is a five-hundred-year-old beautiful and unconventional art form of restoring a broken piece of pottery with lacquer that is mixed with powdered gold, silver, or platinum.

Unlike the traditional response of throwing away a piece of pottery that has been broken, those who practice *kintsugi* restore the broken pieces and artistically give the pottery a new, more beautiful life. Rather than hiding or concealing the damage, the artist carefully mends and transforms the piece into a new unique piece of art. Using lacquer covered with fine gold powder, the broken pottery is celebrated and carefully curated aesthetically back together. *Kintsugi* teaches that beauty is found in the story, in the mess and the brokenness. The damaged pottery is not seen as worthless but it is seen as an opportunity to give the pottery new life, a life that has more value and is seen as more beautiful than before.

> All beautiful things carry distinctions of imperfection. Your wounds and imperfections are your beauty. Like the broken pottery mended with gold, we are all Kintsugi. Its philosophy and art state that breakage and mending are honest parts of a past which should not be hidden. Your wounds and healing are a part of your history; a part of who you are. Every beautiful thing is damaged. You are that beauty; we all are.
>
> —Bryant McGill[3]

Symbolic to this art form, our Savior is the gold that can transform our broken pieces, chips, and flaws into a new beautiful creation. When we lay our brokenness at Christ's feet, he carefully takes those pieces and fills them with His power and grace. He is the artist who transforms us into new beings, beautifully strong and wonderfully made. His grace fills our cracks and makes us whole.

By embracing our brokenness, weaknesses, and inadequacies, we allow Christ into our hearts and souls, allowing Him to do His greatest work.

BY EMBRACING OUR BROKENNESS, WE DON'T COME TO CHRIST'S FEET OCCASIONALLY, BUT WE STAY AT HIS FEET CONTINUOUSLY.

"Yeah, but Tiff, you don't know how cracked I am. I've committed sin I never dreamed I would, I'm in too deep. Too shattered. There's no way I am repairable."

That's simply not true!

If you try to tell me something like this, I have an innate reflex to cover my ears like a three-year-old blabbing nonsense until you stop talking. I don't care if you are shattered into a million pieces that are spread across the world. It doesn't matter. I don't care if you feel that you are irreparable or that you are too far gone or that there is no hope for someone like you.

Lies!

Whatever story you have, no matter what you have done, no matter the sin or how big it is, how deep your addiction, I will look you straight in the eyes and tell you with full confidence that there is absolutely nothing that Christ can't repair.

"What about those pieces that have been shattered because of things that were out of my control? Someone else's choices? What about those broken pieces that I've lost because I was in someone else's hands?" Or, even harder: "What about those shattered pieces of my heart that have happened because my life was in God's hands? Those pieces that have been broken because of the loss of a loved one, sickness, adultery, spouse betrayal, or sexual abuse?"

As much as my heart hurts for those who have been wounded by no choice of their own, I can still say with full confidence that there is no broken heart that is too shattered for Christ. He is a Savior to all. He loves you so much that He would literally hunt this earth on all fours, scouring every last inch of it to find your broken pieces so that He could repair and mend you. His work and His glory is to make you whole. Completely and totally 100 percent changed and renewed into something far more than you could ever imagine being. Sure, it may take Him some time. Sometimes our cracks have become shattered slivers. And it takes longsuffering and patience to mend. But I promise, He can do it. And He will do it!

That's who He is. He transforms ashes to beauty. Who else can do that? Nothing and no one. He is the Master Artist, and if we accept His help, we will become the masterpiece we were meant to be.

Our weakness, flaws, and mistakes don't have to be our story of failure. Instead, they can become His story of redemption. A testament, not of how weak we are, but to how strong He is! Not a reflection of what we did, but what He can do! When we stop trying to hold our broken pieces together and instead fully surrender them and lay them at the Master's feet, we become more than we could ever imagine. Not only that, but for the rest of forever, He is there. If we accidentally chip an edge or some gold lacquer falls out, He is there, mending us every step of the way.

So embrace it, my dear friend. Embrace the mess, flaws, mistakes, and failures. Turn around and stand firm in them. Stop running and own them. Even if you are simply cracked and you don't think it's noticeable enough to fix—take it to Him. Give Him all of you, including your fears, your pain, your heart, and your life. It's OK to not be OK. It doesn't make you a bad Christian. It doesn't make you "less than." It doesn't mean you are failing. It simply means you are experiencing mortality, exactly as you were sent here to do. So let them go; let them fall. Free yourself from holding it together. Embrace the broken.

NOTES

1. Heidi Baker and Rolland Baker, *Reckless Devotion: 365 Days into the Heart of Radical Love* (Bloomington, MN: Chosen Books, 2014), 3.
2. Leonard Cohen, "Anthem," *The Future*, Sony Music Entertainment, 1992, compact disc.
3. Bryant McGill, "Every Beautiful Thing Is Damaged," BryantMcGill.com, accessed June 23, 2017, https://bryantmcgill.com/20141204055135.html.

THIRTEEN

The Voice of Grace

Remember that abusive voice that led my life as a perfectionist? The one who told me I was worthless when I made mistakes and that I would never measure up? I've been told that others hear that voice as well. If they have made mistakes they never thought they would, they are told they are too far gone, too big of a screw up. Friends tell me how that voice tells them that they aren't talented enough, smart enough, or gifted enough. Has that voice ever affected you? Does it let you know every time you have messed up or made a mistake? Does it remind you of all the things you hate about yourself?

That voice is the same voice that wants us to hide our brokenness, to keep it locked up, away from the world. It's the voice that tells you to be ashamed of your body and stay in clothes while your kids have fun swimming. It's the voice that tells you to sit at home and not go to the party because you have nothing to wear. It's the voice that tells you to keep quiet and secret about your sin.

I hate that voice. Freeing ourselves from it isn't easy. It takes time (and is still taking me time), but it's possible. That voice doesn't have to rule your life. Do you know why? Because there is another voice out there that's much, much kinder. A voice that comes from a place of love, hope, forgiveness, and peace. A voice that's quieter than fear, but much more powerful. It's the voice of the Spirit, the voice of Christ's grace.

It is true that fear can have a powerful influence over our actions and behavior. But that influence tends to be temporary and shallow. Fear rarely has the power to change our hearts, and it will never transform us into people who love what is right and who want to obey Heavenly Father.

—Dieter F. Uchtdorf[1]

IN ORDER TO HEAR THE VOICE OF CHRIST'S GRACE, WE MUST MAKE TIME TO HEAR IT. GRACE, LOVE, AND FORGIVENESS COME WHEN WE ARE STILL. WHEREAS, THE VOICE OF FEAR RESIDES IN A CHAOTIC AND FRANTIC ENVIRONMENT.

The greatest blessing that has come from my health trials has been the forced stillness that came with them. While living in the world of perfection, I never had time to just sit and be. Pondering, meditating, listening didn't exist. Even when I was sitting or driving my mind was always to the next two things that I needed to do. My soul was full of turmoil, anxiety, and fear, and these feelings only fed the voice of perfection that told me I wasn't good enough.

For me, relearning how to hear God's voice was essential to changing the way I lived. Every day, I would study my scriptures, read talks, and then practice listening—listening to the Spirit while relearning how to hear it. While I prayed, I often didn't speak but knelt in prayer until I could feel that my mind and soul were silenced. It took a lot of practice, a lot of humility, and a lot of hard work studying the scriptures. Yet every day that I practiced, I felt stronger, and I started recognizing God's voice in a much deeper way. And this transformed how I lived. And what I lived for.

LIVING FROM A PLACE OF KNOWING YOU'RE ALREADY ENOUGH

On the inside of my very first set of scriptures are these words: "We are not human beings having a spiritual experience. We are spiritual beings having a human experience."

These words stung my heart the first time I heard them, and they have continued to do so every time since. Sometimes it is easy to forget that we are so much more than our human selves. And Satan will do anything in his power to make us forget. He doesn't want us to remember that before we came here, we literally walked and talked with God. He doesn't want us to remember how confident we were about coming to earth, because we knew who Christ was. He wants us to believe that we are merely our weak mortal self. But that's not the truth. We are not Man. We are made of the same divine genetics that our own Heavenly Father is, the God that created the heavens and the earth, the God that can move mountains, part seas, raise cities from the ground, heal the blind, and raise the dead. That is who we are. We are His.

One of my very favorite scripture accounts comes from Moses chapter 1. Ever since I was fifteen years old, I have clung to the interaction between Moses and God. In this account, God reveals himself to Moses. God tells Moses: "I have a work for thee, Moses, my son" (Moses 1:6). Then God shows Moses things that are far beyond any mortal or earthly wonder. After this interaction, God withdraws His power and presence from Moses, leaving Moses in an utterly exhausted and mortal state. In his own words, Moses says:

> Now, for this cause I know that man is nothing, which thing I never had supposed.
>
> By now mine own eyes have beheld God; but not my natural, but my spiritual eyes, for my natural eyes could not have beheld; for I should have withered and died in his presence; but his glory was upon me; and I beheld his face, for I was transfigured before him. (Moses 1:10–11)

I thought I understood what this scriptural account taught me when I was fifteen. However, years later, I now know that this amazing interaction gives proof to the amazing, divine, and wonderfully made spirits that we are. Our mortal weakness, failures, flaws, and even our successes don't merit the eternal worth that we have. We are eternal beings who were sent here to have a human experience. We were sent here to be the dust of the earth, so that we may learn and that we may know what is like to be the completely opposite of who we are destined to be.

My favorite part of Moses chapter 1 is when Satan approaches Moses, which Satan seems to do any time one of God's children has a spiritual experience and witness of their divinity. With desperation Satan tempts Moses to worship him.

With full confidence, Moses declares: "Who art thou? For behold, I am a son of God" (Moses 1:13).

What a powerful place to be, knowing exactly who you are and where your worth comes from. Just like Moses, we are sons and daughters of God! He knows your name. He knows what you were sent here to experience.

After everything I thought that I was fell out of my life, I really scrambled to understand how I could possibly have worth when all I could do was sit in bed, day after day. In pleading prayer, I asked God every single day to help me feel of my worth. I remember desperately crying in prayer, asking God who I was now. Who was I when I felt so far from my dreams? Who was I as a woman if I wasn't going to have more kids? Who was I if I wasn't everything that I had ever been good at?

In the most distinguished voice and boldness, the words from Doctrine and Covenants 50:41 echoed in my mind, "Fear not [Tiffany], for you are mine"! At the end of the day, no matter what I have or haven't done, I am God's; I always have been. And so are you. You are not the things that have happened to you. You are not your past, your future, your sins, or even your successes. You are God's, divinely made, and perfectly created. Your worth doesn't come from mortal labels but is deeply woven with the things of eternity. When we accept that, we no longer need to scramble to hold it together to prove we're enough. When we accept that we aren't, we can then have hope in who Christ can make us. When I accepted that I was nothing because of my human and mortal state, the fear of not being enough dissipated and lost its power over me. No longer was I trying so hard to be enough, because I knew that with Christ I am.

Once I finally accepted, like *really accepted*, that (1) I am already enough, (2) that my worth comes from being a daughter of God, and (3) that being mortal, broken, and flawed is a crucial part of mortality, everything changed! When you start living your life being grounded in who you are and *whose* you are, your life becomes powerful. Not easy, but powerful.

> The voice of Grace doesn't allow room for comparison. It knows its success depends on the eyes of God, not on the success and failures of others.

Looking up, which includes seeking a spiritual witness from God, is the only way to understand who we are. The world is utterly incapable of giving us an accurate view of ourselves.

—Sheri Dew[2]

In the past, I often used others as a measuring stick for my own success. Satan had me convinced that if my life didn't look like someone else's, I was failing. I also often looked to see how my own life should be based on how others were living.

"Let's see, she married a doctor, graduated from BYU, went on a mission, and they have five kids."

"You only have one child and she has four . . . you are failing."

"She is a size two and runs marathons. You don't . . . you are failing."

"She has a perfectly clean house while being a full-time mom and business owner. You can't even finish the dishes . . . you are failing."

More lies. That voice that tells you those things? It lies. When I finally committed myself to consistent scripture study, God's voice became much more prominent in my life and everything changed. I now love and have embraced the unique plan that God has for each of us. Perfection for each of us will look different. Christ's grace enhances our unique individuality. Living by His grace doesn't make us the same. In fact, it pushes us further into our own uniqueness. As part of Christ's body, what benefit does God have if we all want to play the same part? He needs us to stand tall in our own path, in our own divine attributes and gifts. He needs us to be perfectly who we already are. That's how God has always worked. Even in the scriptures, can you give me one example of parallel lives?

Noah built an ark; Moses led the Israelites out of bondage; Enoch established Zion; Abraham was asked to sacrifice his only child; Jacob had twelve sons; Daniel tamed a lion; and David was a shepherd who became a king. Each glorified God in a unique and different way.

Just as Eve's life wasn't the same as Esther's, Naomi's, or Mary's, your life isn't going to be the same as your neighbors' or the girl you follow on Instagram. Comparing your life to anyone else's is the most unproductive and derailing thing you can do. Trust me. I used to do it, and it truly is the thief of *all* joy.

God wants your ministry to flow from the realization that you are a beloved child of God. In that place you don't worry too much about how people see you. You don't worry too much about whether they're nice or mean. You don't even worry about whether they love you or hate you. You don't worry because you're simply going to love them and love Him. Your confidence comes from knowing who He is and what He thinks of you. This is what it means to grasp that you are a child of God.

—Heidi Baker[3]

I mean, what if Bruce Wayne grew up idealizing Superman, and rather than discovering his own ability to be a superhero, thought he was worthless because he couldn't be exactly like Superman? Instead of saving the world, what if he sat sulking on a park bench saying, "I can't fly, so I'm basically worthless. It's not fair that Superman got all of these superhuman abilities and I'm just a worthless mortal."

What would our world be like if Bruce Wayne was too upset about not being Superman that he never discovered that he was Batman this entire time! I would imagine God shaking His head, saying, "But I made you the Batmobile, and you're sitting on top of the Batcave!"

As silly as this sounds, how many of us are doing this? How many of us are so upset because of the gifts, talents, and opportunities that someone else has been given that we are sitting on top of our own "Batcave," denying all that God has in store for us as well?

The voice of comparison destroys our worth, but when we stop and choose to listen to the voice of grace, we are led to our own place of power. Together with Christ, we become whole and perfected in our own unique way. There isn't just one right way to live as a Christian. There isn't just one right way to be perfect. Being perfected doesn't mean we will lose our individuality. The scriptures tell us that Moses was a "perfect man." Job was also called a "perfect man." These men were not identical. Just as God used them and their different weaknesses, so is He waiting to use you in a unique and powerful way!

WHEN WE ACCEPT THAT WE'RE ENOUGH AND WE UNDERSTAND HOW MUCH GOD LOVES US, WE ARE THEN ABLE TO LOVE AND SERVE OTHERS IN A DEEPER AND MORE INTIMATE WAY.

I think if all men knew and understood who they are, and were aware of the divine source from whence they came, and of the infinite potential that is part of their inheritance, they would have feelings of kindness and kinship for each other that would change their whole way of living and bring peace on earth.

—Joseph Fielding Smith[4]

It was the first day of a new college semester. I was finally past most of my general credits and was starting into my communication degree. I walked into my first Interpersonal Communication class, sat down, and looked around at the class of about thirty students. My teacher walked in and started handing out a small piece of paper to each student in the classroom. He went to the front of the room, introduced himself, and started covering the class goals and the agenda for the semester.

He then turned around to give us our first assignment.

"OK. For your first assignment, I would like you to write your deepest secret, fear, or trial on this piece of paper."

My heart stopped. The entire room was silent.

He then lifted up a garbage can and said it again.

"I want you to write your deepest secret, fear, or trial on your piece of paper and come and put it in this trash can."

I could hear a few people take a deep breath in. No one moved. And I could feel the fear of our entire class as everyone began getting super uncomfortable. No one looked around, everyone immediately looking down at their desks. *Did he really just ask us to do that?*

"Guys. This is an interpersonal communication class. We're going to dig deep, and to start I need you to complete this assignment. You have two minutes to write something on your piece of paper and then come throw it away in the trash. And I don't want you to write your name on the paper either. Two minutes. Go."

I could feel a slight sense of relief. I mean, we weren't to put our names on the paper and we were putting them in the trash. Slowly I started writing on my paper and could feel as others apprehensively wrote on theirs.

One by one, slowly each student took their piece of paper and threw it in the trash.

Our teacher was standing on the other side of the room, away from the trash can, giving us a sense of semi-peace that maybe the papers would soon be destroyed and no one would see them. Everyone sat down.

"OK, awesome! Thank you."

He then started talking about the depths of each of our lives and the importance of knowing that we all have a story. Then, he did what each and every one of us was terrified he would do. He walked over the trash can, and one-by-one, he took those small pieces of paper out and laid them onto his desk.

Breathing had completely stopped in the room and I could feel the fear and panic. My heart was racing.

Please don't. Please don't. Put them back. Just put them back in the trash.

He sat down. The entire pile of papers in front of him. Then he grabbed one, opened it up, and started to read.

"I have a severe eating disorder and I don't know how to stop."

He grabbed the next. And the next.

"I was sexually abused at eight years old; I have never told a soul."

"My dad walked out on my family when I was twelve. I have never spoke to him again."

"I suffer from extreme anxiety and depression and have been medicated since I was twelve."

"My girlfriend and I messed up and I'm afraid she might be pregnant."

"My parents are on the verge of getting a divorce and I lay awake every night because I can't stop my tears."

"I fear I'll never be loved."

"I am in the depths of a pornography addiction and I'm too afraid to get help."

I was sitting in the back and I could see everyone's head hung low, too afraid and ashamed to look up. My teacher was fighting back tears as he finished each and every last paper. He simply sat there silently, looking at each of us.

"I know this took a lot of courage. But, guys, we all have a story. Every one of us is fighting a demon that feels too big, too unbearable to carry. You, each of you in this room. You are so much more than what you appear. Let's be kind to each other. Let's let love win over judgment. We need each other."

Joseph B. Wirthlin stated:

Love is the beginning, the middle, and the end of the pathway of discipleship. It comforts, counsels, cures, and consoles. It leads us through the valleys of darkness and through the veil of death. . . . Without charity—or the pure love of Christ—whatever else we accomplish matters little. With it, all else becomes vibrant and alive.[5]

That experience in college, although completely terrifying in the moment, changed me. Despite my judgments of those kids in class, once I knew their story, I could never look at them the same. When I understood their brokenness, I loved them. I saw them as my brothers and sisters. I saw them as Christ does.

We have differences. We argue, fight, and contend. But in the end, living by love is the only thing that can change us. Love is the only antidote that can heal broken hearts, broken relationships, broken families, and broken homes. When you love yourself completely as God does, you no longer need to be upset that someone may "have it all together." When you love and forgive yourself for your past mistakes or weaknesses, you no longer feel like others are judging you.

Letting the voice of grace live inside of us not only transforms how we see ourselves but it transforms how we see all of God's children. Truly, we can only love someone else as deep as we allow God and Christ to love us.

WHEN WE ARE OPEN TO HEAR HIS SPIRIT AND PURPOSE FOR OUR LIVES, WE TOO CAN LIVE A CHRISTLIKE LIFE THAT IS STEADY, STILL, PEACEFUL, AND JOYFUL.

Appreciation for our own worth has nothing to do with the applause of one's neighbor and everything to do with having integrity before the Lord.

We all need a higher image of ourselves, but Satan would have us believe it comes totally from the praise of others when in fact it comes from our relationship with God.

—Patricia T. Holland[6]

For years, I let my outward circumstances run my life. Everything that existed on my checklist was directly linked to my self-worth, my perceived value to God, and how successful I was in the world's eyes.

When you live as a perfectionist, everything you do comes from a place of looking at yourself. A perfectionist can stare hours in the mirror finding every flaw. I didn't know I was being self-centered as a perfectionist, but I was. I was so worried about what I was doing, how I was doing it, and where I compared that having a healthy self-esteem wasn't possible. The truth was, I was too worried about my own glory.

During mortality, Jesus Christ knew exactly who He was and what His life's mission consisted of. Because of this, His life was steady, constant, and sound. He never panicked. He never rushed. He was never in a hurry and never had any need to prove to anyone who He was. He knew God's will for Him personally, and everything that He did was to glorify His Father, not Himself. Because everything He did became about God, His worth stayed steady.

Perfectionism is all about glorifying oneself rather than glorifying God. When we stay grounded in our worth, when we choose to please God and glorify Him, we no longer need the world to approve of what we do. We no longer need acceptance from everyone around us. When we focus solely on praising God and glorifying Him, we begin to hear His voice, and that voice overcomes fear.

I don't do this perfectly, but this is now the attitude I try to take every morning. I pray to know God's will for me personally, I pray to know how I can be an instrument in His hands, I pray to be intentional about what goes on my checklist, and I pray for Christ's grace to enable me.

As I too have tried harder to glorify God's will for me rather than my own, I have found greater peace and a greater foundation of self-worth. Do I still have bad days? Yes. In fact, this week I found myself stuck in the mirror because none of my clothes fit and I felt like I was having a hair crisis. However, I quickly realized I felt sad and depressed because, once again, my eyes had shifted from God and back to myself.

When bad days happen, which they do, the first thing I have to do is recognize it. I have to recognize that I've lost control of my own thoughts and that I've allowed insecurities, which are not from God, to reside in my mind. I then immediately cast out the negative thoughts and fear. I demand that they leave. I've discovered that it's a lot harder to fill your mind with positive light when you don't make space for it by casting out the negative. Next, I avoid anything that makes me look inwardly. The scale, the mirror, pictures of myself, social media—anything that triggers my insecurities. I then take action and try hard to lose myself in the service of others. I reach outward in any way I can. Most the time it's simple: I text a friend, write a note to a family member, get down on the floor and play with my son, or (my favorite) I pray! I ask God who needs strength, and then I pray for those names that come to my mind. If I'm still struggling, I bury myself in God's word. I read and study the scriptures until I feel better. This can be just a few minutes or an hour. But eventually, I'm able to enjoy the Spirit again, which in turn gives me hope by helping me to see things in an eternal perspective.

As I've chosen to keep focused on pleasing God, I've been able to let go of unrealistic expectations. I know now that my worth doesn't hinge on my to-do list, or the house we live in, or the business I run. And because of this, I have found freedom. I don't fear failure, I don't fear falling short. I don't care how many Instagram followers I have. I don't worry about what I say, or if someone doesn't like me. I care that I treat people right, but if someone doesn't agree with the decisions I make, I know it doesn't matter.

Through this process, I have learned that a successful day in God's eyes is not the same as a successful day in the world's eyes. I've learned to expect weakness and failure, because this is the learning process, and it's how God keeps us meek, humble, and united with Christ. I've learned that in order to say yes to God, I have to say no to a lot of other things. I've learned that despite my outward circumstances, when I am following my divine personal mission, I am happy.

NOTES

1. Dieter F. Uchtdorf, "Perfect Love Casteth Out Fear," *Ensign*, May 2017, 105.
2. Sheri L. Dew, *Women and the Priesthood: What One Mormon Woman Believes* (Salt Lake City: Deseret Book, 2013).
3. Heidi Baker, *Birthing the Miraculous: The Power of Personal Encounters with God to Change Your Life and the World* (Lake Mary, FL: Charisma House, 2017), 88–89.
4. *Teachings of Presidents of the Church: Joseph Fielding Smith*, (2013), 252–61
5. Joseph B. Wirthlin, "The Great Commandment," *Ensign*, November 2007, 28–30.
6. Patricia T. Holland, "An Eye Single" (Brigham Young University devotional, September 10, 1985), 2, speeches.byu.edu.

FOURTEEN

Pruning Perfection

> Simplified living is about more than doing less. It's being who God
> called us to be, with a wholehearted, single-minded focus. It's walking
> away from innumerable lesser opportunities in favor of the few to
> which we've been called and for which we've been created.
>
> —Bill Hybels[1]

The world. Every time I turn around, there is yet another voice
calling me to come here, be this, do that—telling me that I am
falling behind. The world tells us to go faster, harder, quicker. "If you
don't get your dreams now, you'll regret it. If you don't hustle, someone
else will."

Self-help books are being published by the thousands: be a better
mom, a better wife, get flat abs in five days, grow your Instagram in five
weeks, use social media to make a profit, raise smart and independent
kids, eat organic, live on a farm in the woods. It's overwhelming and
exhausting, and I'm sick of it. I'm sick of Satan telling us that we aren't
enough. Just thinking about it makes my heart ache. It aches for me, for
you, for my children, for your children. It aches for the thousands upon
thousands of people who are being trapped by Satan's suffocating vices
of "be more," "have more," and "do more." I'm straight up tired of him,
his sneaky ways, and his lies. And I'm tired of him taking over our lives!

I am fascinated by the powerful parables that God has intertwined into every beautiful thing that He's created on this earth. His lessons actually live in everything that He's ever touched. If only we would take more time to listen. I'm not a gardener, but I married into a family of green thumbs. One of my favorite benefits of this is the farm-fresh peaches that I get to indulge in every fall. I'm talking about sweet, plump, juicy peaches with juices that drip down your chin when you bite into them. Heaven.

One day while enjoying a peach, I thought about the process and gestation of fruit trees. To survive, fruit trees need more than just water and sunlight. These two positive ingredients are of course essential, but they aren't enough if, as the gardener, you really wanted to be intentional about the fruit you are growing. Weeds are an obvious nuisance to a good fruit tree and absolutely need to be plucked, but still—even doing that isn't enough. To produce the best possible fruit, fruit trees need to be pruned, trimmed, and mended on a consistent basis. This does not include just the damaged branches but (and here is the whole point of all of this) the good branches also need to be trimmed and cut.

> Fruit trees are different from your average shade trees in that they need to be pruned every year to improve fruit quality. Pruning fruit trees is a necessary chore that improves sunlight penetration and increases air movement through the tree. Pruning also develops the structure of the tree so that it can support the crop load.
>
> —Bill Hanlin[2]

It's natural to think, *more branches, more fruit*—right? Wrong. The exact opposite is true. If the branches of a tree aren't pruned, they will begin overgrowing each other, creating an excess of shade that inhibits sunlight. The good branches then bruise and damage each other, making it a prime feeding ground for disease and insect infestation—and eventually, if not taken care of, the overgrowth suffocates the tree, killing its ability to produce fruit altogether. Anyone who has lived in the depths of perfectionism and people-pleasing knows that the symbolism between this analogy and our own lives is uncanny. From a recovering perfectionist who has been addicted to trying to "do it all" her entire life, I can testify that the parable between pruning a fruit tree and the importance of pruning our lives is almost a direct parallel. Believe me, I've lived it.

Growing up I didn't understand boundaries or the importance of being intentional about the things I cut out of my life. I believed the harmful truth that more branches simply equaled more fruit. I was terrified of telling people no; I didn't want anyone to be disappointed in my efforts or to be upset with me. Plus, in my mind, I was supposed to serve others and put others' needs above my own. Right? It's tricky, the way the adversary uses truth, alters it one degree, and leads us to a completely different destination than we intended.

Growing up, I constantly heard that I was part of the "chosen generation," the "latter-day warriors" saved for the last days, that we as the covenant people of the latter days were and are some of God's most righteous spirits. In my little Tiffany world, I believe this meant that we were on the front lines of the war in heaven. I believe that we fought hard and strong for God's plan to come to earth. I believe we were voiced advocates for agency, that we defended it and fought for it, maybe even more than anyone else.

If this is true (and maybe it's only true in my mind), I find it ironic how we, who fought so diligently and valiantly to have agency, are now being placed in a time when there are more choices available to us than ever before. The mass of choices that we face every day is now the very tool that Satan is using against us. The thing that we fought him the hardest on is the very thing he is using to draw our spirits away from the Savior.

Choices and agency are the very things that are destroying us. The challenge of this life is choosing to put God first. In order to fully put Christ first and live by His grace, we have to prune ourselves! It's vital to find time for stillness, for listening, and for pondering. It takes work for Christ to dwell in our heart and mind. It takes pruning and cutting, even the good fruit. But by doing so, we produce the very best fruit possible. Our fruits become equal to the fruits of the gospel: joy, peace, longsuffering, gentleness, goodness, and faith. And don't we all yearn for that?

Christ said to put Him first for a reason. By putting Him first, we are actually putting ourselves first. Yes. Let me say that again. *By putting Christ first, we are actually putting our health and wellness first as well!* You see, when Satan traps us into saying yes to everything and everyone, he eventually leads us down a road were we start saying no to God. For me, saying yes to every opportunity or need of others eventually led me into a life that was so busy that I barely had energy or time to pray, let alone read my scriptures. And ultimately, because I said yes to everyone and everything, I couldn't juggle what I had and ended up letting people down anyway.

> For what is a man advantaged, if he gain the whole world, and lose himself, or be cast away? (Luke 9:25)

It's tough though. In a world that demands our attention in every aspect, a world that yells be more, have more, learn more, and a world that gives us a bajillion and one choices to choose from, how do we prune back? What do we cut out when all the branches seem to be equally good or of importance? The last two years I have found these seven things that have helped me know where to prune and what to prune, especially when it's choosing between two good branches.

1) ASK CHRIST TO STEP IN AND BE OUR GARDENER. (THIS MAY HURT A LITTLE.)

Shortly after Wes and I moved to Arizona, I started my own graphic design business. I had a small niche and clientele built of professional photographers across the nation. This experience was humbling and rewarding for so many reasons. However, as my business took off, so did everything else. Not only was I trying to run a full-time business, but I was also still doing at least two or three side jobs and favors every week. Sometimes it comes with being a designer. There are always jobs and favors that are out there. I was also teaching once a week, training for a triathlon, and on top of it all, I really wanted to start blogging. The trend was kicking off, and I knew I was capable of doing what everyone else seemed to be doing. I was going to elite marketing conferences each year, but I was also watching the blogging world kick off and wanted to be a part of that as well. So "on the side" I was building an online shop and website.

I look back now and just laugh. But there I was trying to be it all and do it all. One night I received an email from a client telling me that they didn't think I knew how to run a business and that I was a flake. The next day I had a friend express their frustrations with me and my inability to answer phone calls or texts. I had family members frustrated with me for not staying in touch. Favors were falling through the cracks. I felt like everyone in the world was frustrated or angry at me. It really hurt. I just wished someone would just give me a break rather than being angry with me. All I was trying to do was be good and help everyone around me. Yet there I sat, upset because it felt like everyone was mad at me.

It can be easy to blame others. And I wanted to—but truthfully, the real problem was me. I was all over the place. Hectic. Frantic. Did I know how to run a business? Yes. I mean, not perfectly, but I was capable. Could I have set up a blog and run an online store and network at all the blogging conferences? Yes. Could I design all the extra favors that people were asking me to do? Yes. Could I be a good friend, mother, and wife? Yes. But I couldn't do all of them all at the same time.

When I asked Christ to step in to be my gardener, it was painful. I know this isn't true, but I almost feel as though He chopped my entire tree back to the root, almost as a do-over. As I started to grow again, there have been times when I've wanted to flourish branches early, forgetting that I was working with a new tree. At the beginning, there were times I was ready to grow branches, but Christ told me it wasn't time, that I wasn't ready.

After all of the change in our family life and careers, Wes and I found ourselves in a spot financially where we needed some more income. I knew I had the capability of starting a business back up, a business that could once again bring us income. I tried four different times to launch something. Each time I prayed and asked God about it, I was told no, that it wasn't time, and that I wasn't ready. For more than three years, Christ asked me to grow slow, that He had something better, and that He would let me know when it was time. Until then, I was told I needed to continue to be still, and that when it was time, Christ would let me know, and together we would grow healthy, stable branches.

So I waited. Instead of earning more money, we cut back. We cut more places in our lives. This was extremely painful. Waiting is hard. It takes a lot of faith. How thankful I am though that I listened. That I've let Christ help me grow those healthy and stable branches. We may grow slowly when Christ is the gardener, but our end result is always worth waiting for. When He is the gardener, we can be sure that every bit of growth is intentional and sustainable. We know we are getting the best fruits.

2) DOES THIS OPPORTUNITY LEAD ME TO CHRIST?

This is now a question I ask myself a lot. It doesn't apply to everything, but in big decisions that I know will occupy a lot of my time, I ask myself this. Does this opportunity take me down a road that will grow healthy, plump fruit that gets me closer to Christ, or does it take away from eternal time too much? Will I have still have time for Christ if I take this opportunity?

> Strength comes not from frantic activity but from being settled on a firm foundation of truth and light. . . .
>
> Let us simplify our lives a little. Let us make the changes necessary to refocus our lives on the sublime beauty of the simple, humble path of Christian discipleship—the path that leads always toward a life of meaning, gladness, and peace.
>
> —Dieter F. Uchtdorf[3]

3) BY SAYING YES TO THIS, WHAT AM I SAYING NO TO?

The fact is, there are only so many hours in a day. We all have to choose how we use them. Whenever I say yes to anything, I always ponder what I will be saying no to. I remember when I was in the hectic stages of my business, I would often complain to Wes how it was overtaking my life. Yet I felt that we needed the money and that since it was a start-up, it was what was required of me to "pay my dues." Granted, any start-up takes a lot of sacrifices. But I truly believed I didn't have a choice. I didn't have a choice to say no. I believed I couldn't say no to family. I believed saying no to friends wasn't kind. I feared that if I said no I would miss out.

> I urge you to clear away the clutter. Take your life back. Use your willpower. Learn to say no to those things that will rob you of your precious time and infringe upon your agency to choose to live in exactness to God's plan of happiness and exaltation.
>
> Don't let the subtle influences of Satan take away any part of your life. Keep it under your own control and operated by your own agency. . . . The path [Jesus Christ] leads us on is not a cluttered path. It is simple and straight and lighted by the Spirit.
>
> —William R. Bradford[4]

Every time we say yes to something, though, we are saying no to something else. If I say yes to constant busyness 24/7, I am saying no to stillness and rest. I was saying yes, yes, yes, to every work problem. The time I committed to those temporal things left no time in my day to ponder eternal things. Because I said yes to my plan, I had no time to say yes to God's plans. Remember that object lesson with the rocks and the sand in the jar? If you try to put the sand in first, you have no room when it's time to put the rocks in. But when you put the rocks in, the sand fills in the empty spaces. When we say yes to God's plans for our day, our to-do list will naturally fall into place.

4) IS THIS CHOICE BEING LED BY PEER-PRESSURE, LED BY FEAR, OR IS IT ACTUALLY BEING LED BY THE SPIRIT?

While in the deepest valleys of my perfectionism, it was easy to get sucked into a mental spiral of accepting and allowing every good thing there is into my life. Even now, as my son is turning the ages where every opportunity is available (soccer, basketball, baseball, year-round club teams, city leagues, gymnastic, piano, swim team, science camp, underwater basket-weaving), I can feel myself starting to get sucked into the feeling that we need him to do everything possible if we want to give him the best possible chance.

But guess what? I refuse to be led by fear and peer-pressure any longer! Because that panic that our child isn't going to be enough if he or she isn't involved in every last thing is driven from fear, the fear of not being enough.

That fear and pressure made me fill my life with so many extra things that were unnecessary. That fear makes us feel like we have to start a business if we want to fit in. That fear makes us feel that we need to attend every social-networking conference in order to be successful. That fear makes us overbook our children with every extracurricular activity possible. But guess what? Filling our lives with every opportunity available is actually destroying our lives altogether. I find a lot more peace in my life when I prayerfully take our extracurricular activities to the Lord. Instead of feeling like I have to sign Jaks up for every single opportunity, I have found that the Lord knows what he needs to develop. The Lord knows his future. The Lord knows Jaks's true passions more than I do. I trust Him to tell me what my son needs to be involved in without sacrificing our lives and time.

God knows what business conferences, parties, speaking engagements, and business opportunities are the most beneficial for you and your family. Take it to Him, let the Spirit guide your decisions, have the courage to say no to the peer-pressure and fear-based choices and say yes to the Spirit-led choices instead.

5) DOES IT, OR WILL IT, BRING JOY INTO MY LIFE?

We all need to remember: men are that they might have joy—not guilt trips!

—Russell M. Nelson[5]

A few years ago, I was talking with a friend who was telling me how hard breastfeeding had been for her. Yet because of fear and pressure that she would be a bad mom if she quit, she stayed with it for a year. This struggle created endless nights of tears for both her and her child. Her sweet baby girl didn't like breastfeeding, and it made it hard on everyone.

How often do we do this? Out of guilt and fear, we force ourselves to do things that the world tells us we should be doing in order to be successful. If there is one thing that God has taught me while living by grace, it's the importance of knowing what makes your own heart beat! God designed and created us to be unique and different—yet so often we compare our own joy with those around us.

One of my favorite quotes is this: "Beauty is whatever gives joy." That beauty looks different for each of us, and when you try to make decision based on what gives someone else joy, you suffocate your own happiness completely. If breastfeeding gives you joy, then do that. If it doesn't, and it's creating tension, resentment, and tears, then don't. If eating paleo, wearing sweats, watching Netflix, having short hair, taking hikes, doing crossfit, or eating donuts makes you happy—then do it! If not, then don't. Find what makes you happy, stand firm in it, and then stop comparing your joy to anyone else's.

I write all of this with the hopes that you understand that I don't mean that any of Gods commandments are flexible. Exact obedience to God's commandments is the key to long lasting joy—however, this doesn't mean we have to do the rest of our lives the exact same. There is no right way to be a good mother. There is no right way to have a successful career. Whatever it is that gives you joy, find it, and live there!

6) IS IT THE RIGHT SEASON?

To every thing there is a season, and a time to every purpose under the heaven. (Ecclesiastes 3:1)

This is so important. I remember constantly feeling so panicked that I was running out of time. Our world shouts from the rooftops that time is short, constantly raising signs to take action now or you'll be left behind. Now, I get this concept. I'm a believer in doing, of getting started right where you are and chasing your dreams. I get the idea that we don't want to be sixty years old, wishing and regretting our lives. But don't you think we will regret missing our lives altogether by chasing after the end?

Chasing after perfection made it impossible to be present in the now. I know I will never regret these past few years of stillness in my life. I have held my son closer than I ever did. I have developed relationships with friends that I never had time for. I have found God and my Savior in the silent, still moments of the day. And really, isn't that all that matters in the end? Our Savior Jesus Christ?

I hate that we feel like the season we are in is never enough. Satan loves to make us feel like we're always falling behind. Maybe you are a stay-at-home mother who feels you aren't doing enough because everyone you follow on Instagram *seems* to be doing more outside the home. Maybe you are a working mom who helps support your family but then also feels guilty that you aren't home *enough*. Maybe you are a father who is tire-lessly working overtime every week just to get by, but feels guilty because you don't have time to coach your sons baseball team.

As my favorite Christian author, Lara Casey, says, "We can't do it all and do it well."[6] And the truth is, we were never meant to. God knows our life. He knows our life expectancy. There will always be enough time to fulfill His will. When we pray to know what we are supposed to focus on in the season we are in, our lives become peaceful. We stop reaching and trying to do too much. Don't be in such a rush to get onto the next season of life that you miss the one you are in. Planting in winters only gives you a unfruitful spring. Don't rush the season you are in, but find hope in God's promise that all seasons of life are yours! The season you are in right now won't last forever. So better or worse, embrace it. And enjoy it!

NOTES

1. Bill Hybels, *Simplify: Ten Practices to Unclutter Your Soul* (Carol Stream, IL: Tyndale Momentum, 2014), 2.
2. Bill Hanlin, "Why Is It Important to Prune Fruit Trees Every Year?" NC Cooperative Extension, accessed June 23, 2017, https://wilkes.ces.ncsu.edu/2013/12/why-is-it-important-to-prune-fruit-trees.
3. Dieter F. Uchtdorf, "Of Things That Matter Most," *Ensign*, November 2010, 22.
4. William R. Bradford, "Unclutter Your Life," *Ensign*, May 1992.
5. Russell M. Nelson, "Perfection Pending," *Ensign*, November 1995.
6. Lara Casey, *Cultivate: A Grace Filled Guide to Growing an Intentional Life* (Nashville, TN: Thomas Nelson, 2017), 38.

FIFTEEN

Finding Joy

It was a crisp spring day in California. The kind of day where the weather is perfect and you can slightly taste the ocean breeze in the air. I rolled down my windows, blared my favorite music, and sang at the top of my lungs. I started laughing, the wind felt good, and I couldn't help but smile. I could feel it, stirring there in my heart, pushing outward toward my face. I started laughing as I turned the music up as loud as my car could handle. Then it hit me. I immediately took another deep breath in to make sure it wasn't a fluke. But there it was, as real as it had ever been: *joy!*

With eyes the size of saucers, I sat there looking up to heaven. My heart felt like it was doing an entire circus routine of excitement. Tears filled my eyes, but this time from happiness. I honestly couldn't recall the last time I had ever felt that feeling. Months ago, I'd doubted I would ever be able to feel joy again. But there it was, so full and real that my heart felt like it could explode. It wasn't fake, forced, or something I had desperately tried to create—it was joy. Raw, innocent, pure joy. Joy that came naturally on its own.

Men are, that they might have joy. (2 Nephi 2:25)

Nothing used to frustrate me more than when others would look at me and tell me that I just needed to be happy, to choose joy, to control my mind and change my attitude. Believe me, if it had been that easy, I would have chosen joy every single day. I wish I could say that I'm the person who wakes up every morning before my alarm even goes off, excitedly jumping out of bed, greeting the day with a huge smile—yeah, no. Ask my husband who knows not to talk to me for the first hour of the day—this isn't the case. For me, joy and happiness take work.

If you meet me in person, you may not believe this. Like I said, I work really hard at being happy and optimistic. But that's the thing: *I work at it*. I have battled extreme anxiety and depression most my life. Between the ages of sixteen and twenty-two, my anxiety was so destructive to my life that I chose to take medication off and on to aid it. Since then, I've also treated myself in a variety of ways, learning all I could to help improve my mental health: counseling, alternative treatment, nutrition—all are tools and external resources that I've learned along the way to help me in my journey to find peace, happiness, and contentment.

I tell you this because I want you to know that I'm not ignorant. The first time I started talking about my journey of finding Christ and the happiness it's brought to my life, I got some initial backlash from others who argued that when you are battling depression and anxiety, you can't just read your scriptures and everything will be fine. Comments like this often make me chuckle. I have never proclaimed that simply reading your scriptures would bring immediate happiness. There are so many things that go into finding joy, especially for someone who battles chronic depression and anxiety.

Mental illness is a real, tangible, and horrible thing. If you have experienced it, you know exactly what I'm talking about. If you haven't, believe me when I say that nothing creates more turmoil than when you desperately want to feel joy, but all you're facing is darkness and sadness. And why would anyone consciously choose that? I would have never ever consciously tried to choose to be miserable beyond measure. So yes, there are certain circumstances that make it extremely difficult to feel joy. I would never deny that. I'm also a huge advocate for counseling, meditating, and any other tool that aids in finding a sound mind. That being said, I also can't deny the power and unfolded joy that has come into my life the last few years while on my journey to finding Christ. His promises are real. They are profound. Not only does His presence in our life bring joy but when His voice is predominately in our mind, He can also lead us to the resources and tools that we need to get help and to find joy. Whether that is via counseling, medication, nutrition, or other treatment options, Christ's truths are sure. When He promises peace, joy, and happiness, He isn't lying. He promises.

As I've lived by Christ's grace, these are the tools that have also helped me find joy every day:

FORGIVE AND LET GO

When we forgive, we set a prisoner free and then discover that the prisoner we set free was us.

—Lewis B. Smedes[1]

This might sound basic, but I have found that forgiveness is key to my happiness. I didn't think I was a person who needed to forgive others frequently. I am usually not easy to offend, and I try hard to give others the benefit of the doubt. But I have found that forgiveness has been a key tool in keeping my mind and heart at peace. I have also found that forgiving something before it even has power to affect me is key to letting things go through the day. If a situation is stressing me out, I will stop and forgive the situation. If I start pounding myself for something I did wrong, I immediately stop and forgive myself. It's not unusual for my day to consist of repetitive forgiveness statements, both in my head and out loud.

I forgive myself for sleeping longer than I wanted to.
I forgive that person for not seeing how those words would affect me.
I forgive my body for not having the energy I wish it had today.
I forgive Jaks for pushing my patience.
I forgive Wes for not noticing that the dishes needed to be unloaded.

Obviously these are some of the smaller things that I say forgiveness statements for. Some offenses and hurt take time. When I've been very hurt, I will find myself needing to forgive over and over in my prayers and throughout the day. However, the more I have exercised forgiving every day, the more freedom I have found, and letting go of things that used to torture me has become so much easier. It's also helped me develop a much deeper love for others and see people the way God does.

God has asked us to forgive, not only because He loves even our offender, but more importantly because He yearns for our hearts and minds to be free. He loves us. And constant forgiveness brings healing and joy.

Every time you forgive, the universe changes; every time you reach out and touch a heart or a life, the world changes; with every kindness and service, seen or unseen, my [God's] purposes are accomplished and nothing will ever be the same again.

—William Paul Young[2]

GRATITUDE

I know gratitude seems like a topic that we talk about a lot. It comes and goes, and it's a simple go-to answer for bad days: "Just count your blessings." Sometimes, culturally as Christians, this simple principle can almost seem too easy to even exercise. But it's true. It's hard to be negative after counting as many blessings as you can. And gratitude can turn even the hardest day into a good day. Shortly after moving to California, I had an experience that shifted my mind and my attitude toward finding the good in the day. I documented this experience in my journal, and I still reference it often:

This morning I woke up completely overcome by the day. My anxiety was high, and I had no desire to even leave the bed. I rolled over, and with a silent plea, I prayed God would give me strength to face the day. Nothing happened immediately, but slowly I got out of bed. I got dressed and I kept moving. When I opened the blinds, I saw that it was raining, gloomy, and overcast. All I wanted to do was crawl back in bed. I said another prayer. Suddenly, with divine help, my hand grabbed Jaks. He was in his pajamas, we didn't have shoes, but I took his hand and we went outside. For the next thirty minutes, we walked up and down our entire apartment complex, jumping in every puddle we could find. I laughed and smiled as I watched his face. It felt good to smile and laugh.

Today I'm thankful for puddle jumping. For little simple things that help me keep moving. I know puddle jumping isn't life changing . . . but maybe it is? Maybe it's the little things like this, each and every day that *do* change lives. I'm thankful for a God who listened and who gave me enough strength to grab my son's hand and find the happy. That moment taught me how important it is to hold tight to the joy of small, simple moments. Pain, heartache, despair, sorrow—these things will always come. But the joy is just as constant, and it is my choice to cling to it wherever I find it.[3]

Gratitude is a powerful principle. I love the way our Savior's life demonstrates the power that can be found when we choose to be thankful. Even Christ's grace is magnified once we choose to have gratitude.

Prior to feeding the multitude, Christ gave thanks for the small bread and fish that they did have. Before raising Lazarus from the dead, Christ prayed to God and gave thanks. This same principle is taught in Paul's life as well. Prior to being miraculously set free from prison, Paul and Silas sang praises to God in their prison cell. That morning the walls of the prison fell and they were set free. These accounts prove the power that resides when we choose to give thanks, even before our prayers have been answered. It may seem simple, but gratitude enhances the power of Christ's grace in our lives, which in turn transforms even our darkest days.

> Gratitude unlocks the fullness of life. It turns what we have into enough, and more. It turns denial into acceptance, chaos to order, confusion to clarity. It can turn a meal into a feast, a house into a home, a stranger into a friend. . . . Gratitude makes sense of our past, brings peace for today, and creates a vision for tomorrow.
>
> —Melody Beattie[4]

PURGE THE POISON

> Saying yes to happiness means learning to say no to things and people that stress you out.
>
> —Thema Davis[5]

This concept is similar to pruning. It's essential, especially if you are struggling with joy. I'm a hypersensitive person. Being in negative situations, watching movies that aren't uplifting, gossiping—it all affects me quickly, and I've learned that creating boundaries and letting go of anything that could hinder the Spirit from being with me is critical.

Purging takes courage, especially if that poison happens to be a friend or family member. Of course, we can't always purge our immediate family, especially if it's a marriage that is struggling; marriage is made up of eternal matter. It takes lots of love, patience, and forgiveness. But if other relationships are causing stress, depression, and conflict in your life, it's OK to take a step back until you find strength to handle those situations.

Lastly, pay attention to those things in your life that bring you down. For me, Facebook is a huge trigger. My spirit is too sensitive, and often the negativity and despair that's prevalent in only a few scrolls brings me down. I can get on every once in a while, but it's definitely a poison that can take me down quickly. I also have found that I'm hypersensitive to most TV shows. I've learned to cut a lot of these things out. We each have different elements that affect us in different ways. Whatever that is for you, take courage to cut it out. Your happiness and joy matter!

FIND WHAT MAKES YOU HAPPY

> May I suggest that you reduce the rush and take a little extra time to get to know yourself better. Walk in nature, watch a sunrise, enjoy God's creations, ponder the truths of the restored gospel, and find out what they mean for you personally. Learn to see yourself as Heavenly Father sees you—as His precious daughter or son with divine potential.
>
> —Dieter F. Uchtdorf[6]

After moving to California, I needed to rediscover who I was. Most of my life, I had lived to please others. I had also believed there was only one perfect way to live a good Christian life, and in the process of trying to mirror this "perfect life," I lost mine. I lost who I was, and I didn't even know what made me happy any more.

> Find out where joy resides, and give it a voice far beyond singing.
>
> —Robert Louis Stevenson[7]

For so many years, I had let outside voices determine what I did or didn't do, that I really didn't know what my own truth and voice was. When I no longer had a business to run, when I couldn't exercise, and I only had one child to take care of, I was left sitting with myself. I desperately needed to remember who I was and where I could find joy.

I decided to challenge myself to do one thing every day that made me happy. I had been numb for so long that feeling joy felt nearly impossible. But I kept at it. Jaks and I drove around looking for new antique stores to explore. We ate strawberries from the farm. I dusted off my bike and rode around the park—not for exercise, but to feel the wind in my face. I cuddled on the couch and watched a movie with my husband. We went to the beach and I simply sat, feet in the water, watching waves come and go. I bought blank white canvases and painted. I designed things on the computer, for no purpose at all—simply to create. I even pulled out my softball glove and went to the park and played catch with my husband.

Doing one thing that made me happy and knowing Jesus became the focus of my life. To someone totally consumed with pleasing others, this seemed selfish. For years I had tried so hard to find success that I had lost myself along the way. I didn't take care of myself. I didn't sleep, shower, or take time for myself. Every part of me was gone. All of a sudden, my choice to make time to be happy started giving me a better life. A life that made me present to the moment. A life of living.

Moments are the molecules that make up eternity!

—Neal A. Maxwell[8]

This exercise became crucial to finding joy again. God doesn't want us to live a life so full of the hustle and bustle that we miss it altogether. He wants us to find joy, every day, even if it's in the simplest of things. I realized taking time for myself wasn't a selfish act, but instead it was important to my personal growth. By taking time to nourish myself, I became a better mom, a better wife, and a better servant of the Lord. So whatever it is that makes you happy, do that. Your happiness matters; it is the very thing that Jesus Christ died for. So find it. Do it. And stop thinking that it doesn't matter. Because it does!

AT THE END OF THE DAY, JOY RESIDES FROM WITHIN, AND CHRIST IS THE ONLY TRUE SOURCE OF HAPPINESS.

Until Jesus Christ is the obsession of your heart, you'll always be looking to mere men to meet needs only He can fill.

—Leslie Ludy[9]

The greatest change that has come from knowing Jesus Christ on an intimate level is the knowledge and understanding that my happiness, joy, and peace can only come from within. When Christ says, "Come unto me . . . and I will give you rest" (Matthew 11:28), He means it. But this rest can only happen from within. And it can only come when we are locked into His reservoir of peace. When I was tied to the Perfect Lie, my happiness and joy were easily affected by my outward circumstances.

When I got married, I even went as far as putting my happiness on the shoulders of my husband.

The truth is, our happiness can only come from within. And it can only come by and through Jesus Christ. He is the way, the truth, and the light. He is lasting happiness. When we spend time focusing on Him, understanding His promises, and letting His love be our source of comfort, His truth becomes our reality. His grace becomes our voice of reason and our lives are filled with immeasurable joy and peace. This doesn't mean we won't have pain and heartache, but it means that the pain and heartache can come and go, and joy and peace can always be ours.

NOTES

1. Lewis B. Smedes, *Forgive and Forget: Healing the Hurts We Don't Deserve*, 1st paperback ed. (New York: HarperCollins, 1996), x.
2. William Paul Young, *The Shack: Where Tragedy Confronts Eternity*, (Newbury Park, CA: Windblown Media, 2007), 235.
3. From the author's personal journal.
4. Melody Beattie, *The Language of Letting Go: Daily Meditations on Codependency* (Center City, MN: Hazelden, 1990), 218.
5. Thema Davis, as quoted in Nikki Martinez, "Learning to Say 'No,'" *Huffington Post*, posted February 23, 2016, http://www.huffingtonpost.com/dr-nikki-martinez-psyd-lcpc/learning-to-say-no_1_b_9294916.html.
6. Dieter F. Uchtdorf, "Of Things That Matter Most," *Ensign*, November 2010, 22.
7. Robert Louis Stevenson, "The Lantern-Bearers," *Scribner's Magazine* 3, no. 2 (1888): 256.
8. Neal A. Maxwell, "The Tugs and Pulls of the World," *Ensign*, November 2000.
9. Leslie Ludy, *Answering the Guy Questions: The Set-Apart Girl's Guide to Relating to the Opposite Sex* (Eugene, OR: Harvest House, 2009), 8.

SIXTEEN

Grow by Grace

At this point, you may be wondering, "So what's really changed, Tiff? What's the difference between your life as a perfectionist and your life now that you're trying to live by Christ's grace?" Well, my friend, *everything.* Everything is changing, because *I* am changing. Does this mean it's all miraculously perfect now? Oh heavens no! In fact, I've realized that the more we come to Jesus, the more we see just how broken we really are and how much we need Him! But now, instead of seeing my cracks with guilt, shame, and discouragement, I see hope. Hope because I know that I'm not the things that happen to me; I am a child of God. Hope in my future. Hope of who I can become with each drop of grace that Christ gives me. And hope that because change is always possible, someday I will be perfected in Christ.

Imagine yourself walking into a large dark warehouse, with only a few flickering lamps spread out across the walls. It's just enough light that you can see the silhouettes of objects within a foot of you. You walk around slowly, but can't make out what's actually around you. Now imagine that, minute by minute, more lights are slowly turned on. As each new light appears, your view of what's around you becomes more detailed and comprehensive. You discover the large object you were resting on was actually an old couch covered in cobwebs and old stains. But then again, as more lights appear, you realize the couch is actually an antiqued Empire sofa with a beautiful damask pattern, something that surely came from the 1800s. With each additional light, your eyes become open to a new level of detail.

It is by this same concept that we grow by Christ's grace. The more we let Him in and the more we receive His light, the more we actually become aware of our true nature and divinity. Without Christ, our full potential is unrealized. Without Christ, we see our weaknesses as dusty old pieces of furniture. But each time we let Christ in, each time we receive Him and His light, our eyes adjust and we see what we are truly made of. We see that despite the scuffs and imperfections, we are without price, and we are open to the possibility of who we can become. No longer do our weaknesses end in discouragement—with Christ our weaknesses become a beautiful opportunity for us to become the perfect eternal beings that we are destined to be.

Perfectionism, on the other hand, hates weaknesses. Instead, it wants us to be flawless immediately and without help. It doesn't want to see the flaws, the cobwebs, or the stains. Perfectionism wants our broken pieces hidden behind perfect, beautiful wrapping—outwardly put together, inwardly shattered. But God would not have it this way. Unlike perfectionism, God knows we will fracture, and there is nothing He loves more than to take us in our mess and change us so that we can have lasting peace, joy, and freedom.

> *Perfectionism is all or nothing.* Growth is little by little. *Perfectionism is all about the goal.* Growth is more about the journey. *Perfectionism is about the outward appearances.* Growth is about what happens on the inside. *Perfectionism is about what we do.* Growth is about who we're becoming.
>
> —Holley Gerth[1]

God is interested in a life that is intentional with long-lasting change. God knows that perfection doesn't come overnight. Our growth is a process and I've learned that God often works slowly. He is not interested in quick fixes or instant gratification. He's interested in growing us step by step, line upon line, and grace by grace. He's interested in permanent, lasting, deep-rooted change. And that kind of growth takes time. It's not an overnight switch, but a daily battle.

Growing by grace is trying, over and over again. It's knowing that we can't be our very best 100 percent of the time. Not even our strengths can be strengths 100 percent of the time. Growth is messy. It's failure. It's days spent in bed. It's messy houses, job losses, hard marriages, being single longer than we had hoped. And it's all the strong, good days in between. Growing by grace is a slow and steady process that involves both our strength and our weaknesses. When we grow by grace, we understand that God is much more concerned with who we are becoming, more than He is concerned about what we are achieving.

My life living as a perfectionist wasn't about change or growth. Instead, it was an illusion; a trap from the adversary that actually distracted me from what was really important! When God allowed my life to crumble, it wasn't because He was heartless or because He didn't love me. No! It was because He *did* love me. God let my life crumble because He wanted me back, and He wanted all of me. He wanted my time, my thoughts, and my heart. He wanted to change me from the inside out.

When everything crumbled, I prayed to get a perfectly healthy body back. But God was more interested in teaching me first how to find my divine worth, self-love, and stillness. While I wanted the big beautiful decorated home—God wanted me to learn how to have gratitude, humility, and contentment. When I thought I wanted five kids, each two years apart, God wanted me to learn how to have faith, trust, and patience. He wanted me to know that life could be joyful, even when it wasn't going as planned.

God loves us, and He knows that we are going to mess up. He doesn't want our failures to shamefully keep us hidden from Him. He wants us to continually come to Him. Especially in our mess and in our brokenness. Because God wants us. And He wants all of us.

> Give me All. I don't want so much of your time and so much of your money and so much of your work: I want You. I have not come to torment your natural self, but to kill it. No half-measures are any good. I don't want to cut off a branch here and a branch there, I want to have the whole tree down. . . . Hand over the whole natural self, all the desires which you think innocent as well as the ones you think wicked—the whole outfit. I will give you a new self instead. In fact, I will give you Myself: my own will shall become yours.
>
> —C. S. Lewis[2]

LIVING BY GRACE MEANS FULLY SURRENDERING OUR WILL FOR GOD'S

I haven't shared this with very many people up until this point, but here it goes. Just over a year before I was given the opportunity to write a book,

I was told that I had a slim to zero chance of getting pregnant naturally. We had been struggling with infertility for more than a few years, and the doctors had finally discovered that my endometriosis was so severe that getting pregnant naturally was not in our books. They also suggested that I get a full hysterectomy, as they couldn't see any alternative in helping me feel better. I was devastated. Knowing we still wanted more children, yet knowing our time was limited, our doctor recommended IVF as soon as possible. This seemed like our last and only option.

I knew IVF was most likely our future, yet, with the money it would require and the injections I would be facing with an already worn-down and exhausted body, I couldn't dismiss giving God one last chance. We knew the odds were against us, but we had faith that if another child was in our future, that God could give us a miracle. We prayed, fasted, and attended the temple. Our families and friends prayed, fasted, and also attended the temple. But after three months, we were still not pregnant. I was heartbroken that our prayers weren't answered the way I would have liked—but I stretched my faith and trusted that (like everything else that had happened) God had a reason.

We continued in prayer and felt that IVF must be the answer. After meeting with our infertility doctor, we moved forward and set a date to begin in vitro.

As the weeks led up to begin treatment, I started having the most horrible feeling. From there, my anxiety only seemed to grow. People told me that it was just because I was nervous about the treatment and that I'd just have to work through the anxiousness. However, in my heart, I knew I was having anxiety for a different reason. I had done hard things before; I knew what it was like to be nervous. I remember how I felt before I had brain surgery. This was different. My heart was starting to tell me that this wasn't the right choice for me, but I didn't understand why. As I expressed my doubt that this was the right decision, people questioned my inspiration, which in turn made me doubt my own inspiration as well.

After the heartbreak of not being able to conceive on our own, why was IVF not feeling right? Having children was a righteous desire. Why was I feeling like this wasn't right either? Only a few days before we were scheduled to start treatment, Wes and I went to the temple. It became clear to both of us that this indeed was not the right choice. I didn't understand. My heart felt broken yet again as I wondered if having more children would ever be right. I left the temple in tears and cried for what felt like the rest of the night.

The very next morning, I received an unexpected phone call. It was from one of the producers at the Mormon Channel. They had found a blog post I had written on *The Small Seed* (a website dedicated to helping others grow their faith that I'd had the privilege of working with for over three years). They had loved my story and invited me to be one of their six presenters for a new series they were launching called *Hope Works*. The series would be patterned after a TED Talk, but focused on faith. I immediately knew that this was an opportunity to share my story in a raw and vulnerable way, and I became overwhelmed with the Spirit as God testified to me that this is why He had said no to IVF.

I was still confused and saddened that we would once again be delaying having another child, but I told God I loved Him, and if this was what He wanted me to do, I would do whatever He asked of me. This experience occupied the next four months of my life, and it became one of my most sacred experiences.

Through these months, Wes and I continued to try and get pregnant naturally, but as the months passed, we still had no luck. Once I was finished with *Hope Works*, we thought it would finally be the right time to put IVF back on the table. But it wasn't.

Again God told me He had a different plan. Weeks went by as I struggled in prayer with the answer I was receiving. Jaks was now almost seven, and the dream of giving him a sibling seemed to be slipping through the cracks. We thought maybe adoption would be the answer instead. But as we headed down that road, it was soon clear that that wasn't right either. God kept telling me to simply wait, even though that was all I felt like I had already been doing.

Well, after weeks of this battle and questioning why I wasn't receiving a yes to IVF, I received an email from Cedar Fort Publishing & Media. They had watched my Hope Works video, and they were interested in giving me a book contract to share my message. I couldn't believe it. Me, write a book? I listened to their offer, and I knew if I accepted, that there would be no way I could start IVF for at least another eight or nine months. Yet I could feel the Spirit pushing and prompting me, whispering that this is, again, why God had told me no.

It didn't seem fair, and in my weakness, it felt as though God was asking me to give up having more children altogether. I was intimidated by the deadline. I was overwhelmed at the task. And my heart just wanted another baby. For two weeks I wrestled with God. Everything felt against me. It was all too much. I asked God if there was any other way. I told

Him that He had the wrong person, that surely there was someone else who could write these words. And I'm sure there was. "For many are called, but few are chosen" (Matthew 22:14).

Again, I could hear the Spirit and God's voice. "Do you love me, Tiff? Do you trust me, Tiff? I have not led you this far only to lead you astray. Have faith. You can hand it over to me. Hand me your will. I promise I have a plan."

Despite all the logical reasons why writing this book seemed to not make sense, I knew it was what God was asking me to do. And I knew to do God's will, I had to hand over my own. I had to hand over my will of wanting another child right now. I had to hand over the fear that Jaks may be our only child. I had to hand over the anxiety that no one would even buy a copy of the book. I had to hand over the insecurities, the fears, the unknown.

And I did. Granted, I didn't do it very gracefully. There were a lot of tears. But I signed the book contract, and I knew that it was what God wanted me to do. And that obedience became the sole reason behind writing this book.

Choosing Jesus Christ and God isn't always easy. Discipleship is hard, stretching, and the most humbling work you'll ever do. It requires stripping down every last piece of our pride and selfishness. But, in the end, it's worth it. Because when you completely and totally love Jesus, it really isn't a sacrifice at all. Although I felt like I was choosing the harder path, once I turned it over, once I jumped, God caught me. He has carried me. Slowly I have seen how His path wasn't as hard as I thought it would be. It's been hard, but there has been joy in places I didn't think I could ever find joy. Once I surrendered, God gave me peace about my infertility. I started finding joy in sharing my story with others, and I have been surrounded with more love, support, and comfort these last few months than I could have ever imagined. Through this process, God has once again proven that Christ's grace is indeed sufficient. And it's been a beautiful amazing miracle to witness.

After a strenuous and intense deadline of writing, I was successfully able to hand in my manuscript on time. As the next few weeks went by and I waited for the first round of edits, I became extremely sick. I attributed it to my system crashing after writing and reliving the hardest parts of my life. But as each week passed, it wasn't letting up. I couldn't get out of bed. I felt like I had a flu that wouldn't go away. I started throwing up a few times, and it felt like I had been hit by a train. I couldn't figure it out.

My edits were coming back, and I was having the hardest time working through them. It was as if I had been totally compromised. I couldn't think straight; I couldn't write. Words were no longer coming to me.

After spending two days desperately trying to push through with no luck, I called Wes telling him I needed to go see the doctor. I assumed maybe my thyroid was off, or maybe I had celiac. I heard Wes start to talk and then stop. Finally, he said, "Tiff, are you pregnant?"

I dropped the phone. It couldn't be. Once I had moved on and dove into my book, I had removed even the thought of having another child from my mind altogether. I had come to terms with the fact that it might not be in the cards for us and I had let go of it. I hadn't considered pregnancy as an explanation at all.

"Tiff? Tiff!"

I frantically found the phone and picked it back up.

"Sorry. I just— I don't think— Maybe. Do you think? Umm, wow. Yeah. I guess I *am* late. But I couldn't be. Not now! Not now that I'm in the depths of this book process!"

In the most gentle way he could, without sounding too anxious, Wes suggested that maybe I take a pregnancy test, just to make sure.

I couldn't breathe or think. I tried brushing it off and attempted to keep working. But my heart was racing and I couldn't get it off my mind.

Wes called me again. "Tiff, wouldn't you rather know than keep feeling so anxious?"

I didn't know if I did. I mean, I felt anxious either way. What if the test said no? Again. But then, what if it said yes? I couldn't wrap my head around it. The timing. The miracle. The fact that maybe the answer finally was yes. After a lot of prodding, I finally agreed. Three positives later, I accepted it. I was pregnant.

Faith is a funny thing. Sometimes it feels like we are giving up so much for God. It feels like His timing never makes sense and His ways are never predictable. But God is good. Oh, how I know that. What a testimony this sweet miracle has been for me in the middle of my mess, when I least expected it.

Did I think this would be the outcome I would be blessed with when I surrendered my will months ago? No. I had accepted the painful truth that maybe my desires, however righteous, were not part of the Lord's plan for me. It was a hard thing to let go of, but I did it because the Lord asked it of me. It's crazy how sometimes we are blessed with the desires of our hearts, once we finally hand it to God. That isn't to say that this will always happen. Sometimes those promises don't come to pass until the next life. But the point is, even when we feel like God isn't answering, He is. God always keeps His promises. And He is always good, even if we don't understand.

Which is funny, because even as I write this, I can feel it. That little twinge of doubt. Wondering if this is what I should have shared. Should I have shared that I am pregnant? Should I have shared this part of my story? I'm only ten weeks along. What if things don't work out? The future is still unknown.

I guess this is just proof that I'm still learning. I'm still growing and learning to trust the very words I write. But that is what living by Christ's grace really is. It's letting go of the unknown future, even when we have doubts. It's surrendering our will, and fully trusting that God has us, even when we can't see it. And it's finding peace that everything really will be OK, no matter the outcome. Because no matter what happens, no matter how hard the trial is. We always have Jesus. And as long as we have Him, everything really is OK.

SO HERE I STAND, EMBRACING MY BROKEN MESS, INVITING YOU TO DO THE SAME

I hope that you know that God loves you. He is aware of you in this moment, however that looks. Maybe you are reading this in the quiet chambers of your room, in sweats and a T-shirt. Maybe you are between flights at the airport, or in a hospital room caring for a loved one. Wherever you are, whatever condition you are in, God knows. And He wants you. All of you.

He wants you in your strong empowered moments and in your anger. He wants you when can't go another step and are lost in tears. You are His, and you are mighty! Even in your brokenness.

"But, Tiff, you don't know what my brokenness looks like. There are a lot of pieces."

You're right. I don't. But Christ does. You may have a million pieces spread across the world, or you may simply feel cracked. It doesn't matter, because He knows. And while Christ may be the only one who truly understands what you are experiencing beneath the skin, that doesn't mean that I don't want to try. Because deep down, we need each other. We need to know each other's struggles and trials. We need more love and less judgment. More truth and fewer perfect facades. And we need hope—hope that we aren't alone.

So here I stand, in my vulnerable mess and shattered pieces, asking you, "Will you join me?" As your sister in the gospel of Jesus Christ, can we unite in purpose, truthfully and vulnerably? I may not know you personally, but I know Him. I know your Savior, because He is mine. And you're right, our journey isn't the same, but our destination is. And that, right there, is a good enough reason for us to join arms, don't you think?

So while I'm here picking up my pieces and finding Christ—I want you to know that I'm cheering you on while you pick up yours. I know what a painful process it can be to look at the shards of a past self, and I know that I have survived because of the good people that have cheered me on. And I'd like you to know that someone is doing the same for you.

Christ is waiting with arms wide open, ready to embrace all that you are. He is ready to transform you. He is ready to make your life more than you could ever imagine. He is ready to give you a life of peace, hope, stillness, and joy! A life that extends far beyond the hustle and bustle of the world.

But the truth is, He can't if you don't come. And He can't if you don't lay it at His feet willingly. He won't compromise your agency, but His love, joy, and grace are waiting. Those blessings are already yours, and Christ is ready to give you His power if you want it. So surrender, my friend. Surrender. It's OK, I promise. Breathe in, breathe out. Stop hiding and embrace it. Every last piece of it.

NOTES

1. Holley Gerth, *You're Already Amazing: Embracing Who You Are, Becoming All God Created You to Be* (Grand Rapids, MI: Revell, 2012), 46; italics in original.
2. C. S. Lewis, Mere Christianity, rev. ed. (1952; repr., New York: HarperOne, 2001), 196–97.

Acknowledgments

They say that it takes a village to raise a child, but after writing this book, I've learned that it takes a village to do anything worthwhile in this world. My gratitude and thankful heart could bleed onto a million pages. There is no way I could ever give adequate thanks to the hundreds of people who have made this book possible—family, loved ones, friends, and even strangers. Thank you. Thank you to each of you who have shown up in my life, exactly when I needed you. Thank you for the messages, the calls, and the hugs—each one of them came when I needed that extra strength to keep going.

Mom and Dad, I could have never done this without you. Thank you for showing me perfect love as you continue to love me, even in my shattered mess. Without your countless sacrifices and endless service to ease my stress, I would have never met my deadline. Anything that I am, is because of who you are.

McKell Parsons, thank you for believing I had a message worth writing and for giving this book a chance. Katy Watkins, not only have you given my words the added strength they needed but you became a fast friend and an encouraging voice, exactly when I needed it. And Kaitlin Barwick, thank you for adding your talents and giving my book the perfect finishing touch.

Michelle Torsak, Raven Ngatuvai, and Irinna Danielson, I still get tears every time I think about each of you. Thanks for taking a chance on a hott mess who loves her yoga pants.

Wesley Paul, there are never any words. You've been the constant encourager, the shoulder I continually cry on, and my number one fan.

Acknowledgments

Without you being my rock, we both know I wouldn't have finished. What a journey it's been. I love you forever.

To my favorite sidekick and greatest joy, Jakston. I love you more than my heart can handle. Thank you for your endless patience. May you forever know that your mom knows that Jesus Christ is the only way to be happy. He loves you. God loves you. I love you. Don't ever forget that your worth comes from being a son of God.

And of course, to my Savior Jesus Christ, and my beloved Heavenly Father. I am humbled to have been an instrument in your hands. Thank you for teaching me that your grace, strength, and love are truly sufficient, and thank you for showing me that even the weakest things of this earth can be used for good. May my life forever be dedicated to serving you. I love you!

About the Author

Tiffany is a writer, speaker, and designer who believes in letting go of perfection, embracing the broken, and living intentionally by the powers of grace. Tiffany graduated from Dixie State University as a duo athlete and with a BA in communications and public relations.

After years of struggling with perfectionism, anxiety, and depression, God broke everything Tiffany had and called her to His feet. Battling multiple chronic health issues, including infertility, she closed the doors to her full-time design business and with a renewed determination she devoted her life to finding Christ and seeking wholeness.

It is now her mission to help others know their Savior, Jesus Christ, so they too can feel the healing and peace that comes from His infinite Atonement. To accompany this, Tiffany has founded Evergreen—a unique community and website that's dedicated to helping others become rooted in Christ through inspiring study guides, tools, and resources.

Tiffany currently lives in Southern Utah with the man who gives her wings to fly and their one perfect son who makes her world go 'round.

HEY—LET'S BE FRIENDS!

Thank you again for sharing my journey with me. I really hope someday we can sit down and have lunch together. Until then, I'd love to connect with you in other ways.

- Come visit me at **TiffanyWebster.com** and follow along as I share more of my journey of learning to live day by day in His grace.
- Or, of course, come say hi and connect with me on Instagram: www.instagram.com/tiffany.webster

COME JOIN THE EVERGREEN COMMUNITY!

Having faith in Christ is not a one-time event, but something that should be kept fresh and alive each and every day. Evergreen's purpose is to provide beautiful tools and resources and a community that supports you on your personal journey of finding Christ.

For as we *seek* Christ and *partake* of Christ, we *become* like Christ.

- To learn more about Evergreen or to download our free resources and study guides, visit us at **BecomeEvergreen.com**

Scan to visit

www.tiffanywebster.com

CPSIA information can be obtained
at www.ICGtesting.com
Printed in the USA
BVHW030309181218
535863BV00036B/721/P